The Building Blocks *of Success*

Focus On the Fundamentals and Be Successful at Everything You Do

Bobby G. Muse Jr.

The Building Blocks of Success

Simple Life Publishing
Louisville, KY
www.SimpleLifePublishing.com

ISBN: 0615741398
ISBN-13: 9780615741390
LCCN: 2013900305

"All our dreams can come true…
if we have the courage to pursue them."

Walt Disney

Acknowledgments

To my wife and best friend, Mary, who, while always encouraging me to do my best, allowed me to sit for hours on end in front of a computer to follow a dream.

To my kids Jonathan and Kristen, who taught me more about success than any business school could ever teach me.

To my good friend Teresa Arthur Kappner for her time invested in proofreading and providing invaluable suggestions to this effort.

To my family, whose love and understanding has made this book possible.

Table of Contents

Introduction

Believe it or not, being successful at anything in life is not difficult. In fact, it is scary how simple it really is when you fully understand what it takes to be successful. When you break success down into its fundamental elements and begin to focus on the things that are really important to being successful, success comes naturally.

Not only is being successful easy once you understand what is involved, anyone can be successful. Success doesn't depend on your socioeconomic status, nationality, gender, or race. If you have a good idea or dream you want to develop or follow and you pay close attention to the fundamentals of success, you can be successful at anything.

When we break success down into its fundamental elements it unclutters the process and simplifies our path to success. How does this happen? We falsely believe that to be successful at anything the process has to be complicated. We've heard all our lives that nothing worth accomplishing is ever easy. As a result, shortly after we conceive an idea, we convince ourselves that we're not qualified to accomplish what we want to achieve, not smart enough to understand what is involved, or because of its perceived complexity, we don't have enough time or energy to even try. What do we do? We talk ourselves out of trying before we even get started. Remove that thought from your head immediately! There is nothing further from the truth. Simplicity is the key to everything in life. The simpler anything is, the easier it is to achieve. Keeping the process as simple as you can by breaking it down into its most fundamental elements is the key to being successful at everything.

When I say breaking everything down into it most fundamental elements, I'm not talking about traditional goal setting. If you have ever taken a class on goal setting, you'll know that instructors often have participants break every goal down into its smallest tasks. Breaking every task of an overall goal down into its smallest tasks, they reason, makes the goal easier to accomplish. That is not what I am talking about here when I say fundamental elements. I'm not talking about breaking everything down into a thousand tasks you need to complete at one at a time.

So, if I am not talking about goal setting, what am I talking about? I'm talking about the basics of success. I'm talking about staying focused on the basic elements that are inherent to being successful in everything you do. Please don't misunderstand; identifying tasks you need to complete to accomplish a goal is important, but there is an even more basic set of elements necessary for you to be successful in everything you do.

Why does the traditional goal setting process fail for many people? Because even as simple and logical as this process may sound, it is too complicated, time consuming, and not a natural fit for everybody. Not everyone's brain is wired this way. I have found most people end up so consumed by the process of breaking every goal down into its smallest task that they lose focus of their overall goal and then fail. The execution of the process becomes more important than the overall goal they are trying to accomplish.

What are the fundamental elements I am talking about? When you break success down into its simplest form, there are seven fundamental elements that you must stay focused on to be successful. Although we will spend more time on each one later in the book, the first element is that you must commit yourself to being successful. Whatever you strive to accomplish, you must be committed to doing your best. Success doesn't come by just saying you want to be successful at something; you must stay focused on your goal and want it bad enough to make it a top-level priority in your life.

Second, you must believe in yourself. If you don't believe in yourself, you will never be as successful as you could have been. Success depends on your confidence in yourself and your ability to do the things necessary to accomplish your goal.

Third, you must develop a winning attitude. Now I'm not talking about a positive attitude. No one can have a positive attitude all the time, and although it will lull you into thinking things are going great, just having a positive attitude will not make you successful. To be successful you must develop a winning attitude that doesn't allow you to be defeated.

Fourth, you must be adaptable. The world we live in is ever changing. In the computer industry, something introduced today is obsolete in six months. To be successful, you must adapt and make the most out of every situation.

Fifth, you must continually learn new things. If you stop learning, the world and your dreams will leave you behind. Knowledge is power and provides the tools that make being successful possible.

Sixth, you must train yourself to think outside the lines. A young child doesn't color inside the lines, and neither should you. Not until we, as parents, force our children to stay within the lines of the drawing, do they begin to do so. Why is this bad? Telling them to stay inside the lines creates a confining standard that limits their creativity and thinking. To be successful you must avoid letting yourself or others draw lines around you. You must think outside the lines whenever necessary.

Finally, you must tell everyone you come in contact with about your goals and dreams. Why? Because there are multitudes of people out there willing to help you. That's right; people want to help you be successful. However, to find these people and garner the help you may need, you have to tell everyone you meet, because you never know who is willing to help.

If you stay focused on these seven fundamentals of success, they will not only make accomplishing your goals and dreams simpler by uncomplicating the process, but they will also make it easier to find success in everything you do.

Focusing on the seven fundamentals of success makes being successful easier, and all of us have already been exposed to and have partially developed these attributes within ourselves by the age of thirteen. By this time, we already have been introduced to the skills we need to be successful in every aspect of our lives. Most of these skills—attitude, determination, steadfastness, adaptability, persistence, and self-value—were fully developed by the time we were teenagers. How can this be? It's easy; growing up and developing through our childhood years exposed us to every fundamental required to be successful.

Regrettably, somewhere between childhood and adulthood, many of us forget how to be successful. The determination and drive that got us through the first few years of life is erased from our conscious minds and is forgotten. We forget how to overcome the simplest of obstacles. We forget how to adapt and refuse to accept new ideas. We lose confidence in ourselves and believe we are not in control of our own destinies. For whatever reason, we erase from our minds the skills that helped us mature as children to reach our potential and that helped us develop into who we are today.

Even though the potential for success is present within all of us, we make reaching our potential much more difficult than it really is. We are a society of people drifting aimlessly, not content with who or where we are and not believing we can do anything about it. We are not happy with the way things are going with our lives, but we are not dissatisfied enough to do something about it. As I stated before, we convince ourselves that we are under qualified, the tasks are too large to overcome, or we don't have the time to accomplish what we really want to do. Consequently, we do nothing. We give up before we even try. We lose sight of our goals and dreams and drift aimlessly through life without reaching our full potential.

Children, on the other hand, even with their limited knowledge of life at the time, understand how to be successful. They are confident in themselves and are convinced they can do anything. They rarely give up or even consider failure. Children don't care if they are qualified. If there is something they really want to do, nothing will stop them. Not even their parents can keep them from attempting something that is important to them. They don't give a second thought about or even try to anticipate the possible problems that might arise. They push forward, work through the problems as they encounter them, and never look back. Unlike adults, children usually find time to do something they really want to do.

Children are great teachers of life and success. In just a few short years, children overcome countless obstacles to become successful at many things. They learn to scoot, crawl, walk, and then run. They develop language skills and begin to communicate with others. They learn to feed, dress, and bathe themselves. They learn their ABCs and begin to read. They learn to count to one hundred and do simple math. Each step of the maturing process is a success story in and of itself.

The following chapters reintroduce you to the seven fundamentals of success and teach you to refocus your efforts, allowing you to be successful at everything you do. These fundamentals are not new or revolutionary. As I illustrate through examples of my children—Jonathan and Kristen—they are the same skills that all of us developed to be successful as children. I am convinced that the fundamentals that made us successful as children can and do make us successful as adults.

Each chapter describes in detail one of the fundamental elements. As we go through the book, I relate how my children used these same fundamentals to overcome obstacles to their development and become successful as children. These are the same fundamentals we use as adults to be successful at everything we attempt in life. By focusing our efforts on these seven fundamentals, we simplify the process of being successful into its most basic essential elements, the building blocks of success. At the end of each chapter, apply these fundamentals to the obstacles that keep you from reaching your full potential, and begin to find success in everything you do.

I hope that through this book you can once again find the characteristics that made you a successful child and apply them to your life as an adult. Focusing on these seven fundamentals of success will make you more successful than you ever dreamed. Allow them to build your character and make you successful in everything you do.

Turn the page, and let's get started.

What Do You Dream About?

We all have ideas, dreams, and aspirations. We all have goals we want to accomplish. We all have things we want to achieve while we are here on this earth. Some are as simple as losing ten pounds or as complex as becoming the CEO of a large corporation. For whatever reason, sometimes these dreams remain abstract and never realize their potential. They are pushed into the "someday" part of our mind where they remain locked in a room and are never given the opportunity to flourish and grow.

Children, just like adults, dream about what they want to do or who they want to be. They visualize themselves as doctors, nurses, lawyers, firefighters, famous athletes, rock stars, ballerinas, the president, or a multitude of other people. They imagine themselves in the future having fun doing things they think will make them happy. To children, having fun and being happy are the most important things in life.

Both my children had vivid dreams of what they wanted to do someday. My son, Jonathan, from the moment he was able to verbalize his dreams, dreamt of becoming an engineer or an astronaut. Some of us know at an early age what makes us happy and we live our entire lives following those dreams. Jonathan is one of those people. In the twenty-nine years since his birth, his dream has never wavered.

His love of science and math helped shape his life, and it continues to keep him focused today. His thirst for knowledge remains as unquenchable as it was when he was a child. I'll go into more detail later, but Jonathan had to know how everything worked. If an item did something, he wanted to know how. He was constantly asking questions of those around him and taking things apart to see what made them work.

Kristen's dreams, on the other hand, have not been as defined as Jonathan's have and grew a little each day. Unlike her brother, her dreams have changed from time to time to meet her needs at a particular point in her life. She has never stayed on one dream too long, but is constantly looking for the thing that will meet her needs and make her the happiest.

Kristen is a caring and sensitive girl, who is most often thinking about people who are less fortunate. As a little girl, she prayed daily for the homeless and the poor. She was often thinking about the sick and those in hospitals, hoping they would get well soon. Kristen is a very social person, and helping others gives her life meaning.

One evening just before bedtime Kristen and I talked about her dreams and about what she wanted to be when she grew up. Not knowing what to expect, I listened closely as she responded to me in as serious a voice as she could. "Daddy, I want to be a school crossing guard when I grow up," she said. Now don't get me wrong; I don't have anything against school crossing guards. They provide an essential service for little pay. Although Kristen expressing her desire to become a school crossing guard was consistent with her desire to help others, it caught me a little off guard and was not what I expected her to say. I assumed her dreams would be much bigger and more grandiose. I thought she would want to be a doctor and treat indigent people in the inner city. I thought she would want to be a public defender and represent people who couldn't afford a lawyer. I thought she would be a special education teacher who helped children with learning disabilities. But Kristen, at that point in her life, didn't consider those vocations at all. She wanted to be a school crossing guard and there was no talking her out of it.

Her observations of the crossing guard at her school convinced Kristen to pursue that as a career. She was impressed with the friendliness and respect the officer received as he stopped traffic to help students cross a busy street. In her own mind, she reasoned that this job would not only help others, but would also be a fun job that would provide her much happiness.

Fortunately for Kristen, later that same year she got a taste of her fun job. Appointed to a safety-patrol student position at her school, she helped students get to where they were going before and after school. Kristen quickly learned that the job was more difficult than she first thought and was not as fun as she had hoped it would be. She was astonished at how unappreciative other children were when she tried to assist them. As a result of her experience, her dreams changed again, and she decided she wanted to own a pet store to surround herself with animals of every kind. Unlike Jonathan, as Kristen matured, so did her dreams.

Adults are like children when it comes to dreams. Just like Jonathan, some of us know early on what we want to do with our lives. We know what will make us happy, and we never stray far from it. Others of us, like Kristen, are continually looking for things that will make us happy. We search throughout our lives looking for something we are not sure we will ever find.

Although adults and children are similar in the way they approach their dreams, children are much different in the way they chase them. Children live their dreams. Children act out their dreams. Children don't allow their dreams to remain locked up in their minds to never be pursued. To children, "someday" is today, and once they think they know what will make them happy, they set into motion chasing their dream.

Even though they have limited knowledge about what is involved in accomplishing their dreams, they attempt to incorporate their dreams into their play and life. They pretend and act out their dreams with friends as they build forts, playhouses, and other structures where they can make believe. They create imaginary friends to share their adventures and fun. They watch TV and movies about topics that are similar to their dreams and hopes. They rarely miss an opportunity to make their dreams come alive in their daily lives.

Adults, on the other hand, seldom pursue their dreams. They sit back and rarely allow their dreams to come alive in their daily living. Their dreams never become concrete but stay abstract—sometimes never moving beyond the planning stage. They remain locked up within their minds, never to be acted on.

For some people it takes a catastrophic event to unlock their dreams and move them to action. A death, a serious accident or illness, a job loss, or some other substantial event is the only thing that gets their attention and makes them stop what they are doing and reevaluate their priorities. Until this happens, they keep their dreams locked up in their minds until something shakes the dreams loose. Unfortunately, and this is important, those who never live their dreams will never achieve them.

Sometimes adults let others take our dreams from us. We allow unimportant things to clutter our lives and distract us from our hopes and dreams. We become involved in activities—in and outside of work—that dominate our time and sidetrack us from things that make us happy. We allow organizations that we belong to demand more time from us than we anticipated or feel comfortable giving. We agree to take on tasks that require more of our time than we are sometimes willing to give. We complain about our lack of time and say "if we only had twenty-six hours in a day" we would have all the time we needed to do everything we wanted to do. Unless the earth's rotational axis changes at some point, we continue to be limited to twenty-four hours a day. Successful people find the time to do the necessary things with the available time allotted to them.

Others of us become couch vegetables that must be entertained every free minute. We lay on couches staring blindly into picture tubes, accepting almost everything presented to us. With remote controls molded into the palms of our hands, we surf channels, living our lives through other people. In the midst of the clutter, our dreams distort and we lose focus on our hopes and goals. Those of us who are successful in this world are the doers in life. Successful people live their dreams.

What do you dream about? What makes you happy? What have you always wanted to do that you have only thought about doing? What aspirations do you have that have never realized their potential but have been pushed into the back of your mind? Do you fantasize about starting a business? Do you visualize losing the weight that you gained since high school? Do you imagine changing jobs or going back to college to start a new career? Do you envision going to see a relative in a distant city that you haven't seen in years? Do you daydream about relocating to your favorite beach resort or cabin in the mountains? Do you think about going on a trip around the world? What about running for public office or writing a best seller that breaks all publishing records? What are your dreams?

It's good to dream. It's good to remove ourselves from the daily clutter of our lives and evaluate where we are and where we want to go. It's a good time to put our lives and goals in perspective. However, to be successful at anything, dreaming must always be followed by action. Carl Sandburg, an American poet and winner of three Pulitzer Prizes said, "Nothing happens unless first a dream." Without action, dreams remain abstract and never become concrete. They remain in our minds, and we never allow them to flourish or grow.

When our son Jonathan was five years old, my wife and I bought him a pair of walkie-talkies—a pair of inexpensive radios that cost about twenty dollars. They worked fairly well at first, but like any other inexpensive toy, one of the units quit working. My son was devastated. His prized toy that allowed him to secretly communicate with his friends was broken.

After it broke, Jonathan must have turned his broken walkie-talkie off and on a hundred times trying to make it work. It never did. The frustration on his face each time he turned the radio on said it all. He was determined to make it work.

A short time later, I found him in his bedroom with his radio spread all over the floor. He must have had it broken down into twenty or thirty pieces. Knobs, circuit boards, and wires were everywhere. My first reaction was to scold him, but after a quick reevaluation, I decided against it. I decided to let him try to fix it. What would it hurt? If I didn't let him try, I was almost certain that I would never hear the end of it. As I left his room, I tried to prepare him as easily as I could for disappointment by suggesting to him that he was wasting his time and shouldn't bother trying to fix it. In hindsight, that was a mistake.

Little did I know that disappointment was the furthermost thought from Jonathan's mind. He wasn't at all worried about being able to fix his radio. You see; it didn't matter to him that he didn't know anything about transistor radios. It didn't matter to him that I thought he was wasting his time. It didn't matter to Jonathan that my wife and I were having a good laugh in the kitchen at his expense. He wanted his walkie-talkie to work so that he could have fun with his friends. That's all that mattered to him.

For the next two days, it was next to impossible to remove Jonathan from his room. He spent every waking moment working on his walkie-talkie. He stopped playing with his friends. He didn't watch his favorite television programs with his family. In fact, my wife and I had a terrible time just getting him to eat. He had made it perfectly clear to us that fixing his walkie-talkie was the most important thing in his life at that time, and nothing was going to keep him from it.

Just as I started to worry about Jonathan's obsession to fix his walkie-talkie, he met me at the door one day as I came home from work. With a big smile on his face, he told me that he had something to show me. He gave me one of his walkie-talkies, turned it on, and asked me to listen. He left the room, and a few seconds later I heard his voice break through the static on the radio. "Can you hear me dad?" he asked. "Can you hear me?"

Jonathan was ecstatic! He had every right to be. He had taken a very limited knowledge of electronics, endured ridicule from his parents, and didn't allow distractions around him disrupt his ultimate goal of fixing his walkie-talkie. He didn't stop and rationalize his possibilities for failure. I'm sure he never even considered failing. He knew in his heart before he started that he was going to fix his walkie-talkie no matter what he had to do.

Unfortunately, most adults never focus on the possibility of succeeding, but dwell on the possibility of failing. As we get older, we let our defeatist reasoning control our lives and reduce our dreams to passing wishful thoughts when we stop to consider the possible difficulties we might encounter along the way. As a result, we never try. We give up and accept defeat before we even start.

So what keeps us from trying? What causes us to believe we can never be successful at something before we try? When it comes to success, the biggest challenge we face is ourselves. We are our own worst enemy. We let our keen ability to think and rationalize talk us out of doing many things before we even start. How? Here are five ways:

First, we let memories of past failures bombard our minds and keep us from trying. We think about all the things that have happened in the past that didn't go as we had planned. We remember past mistakes that ruined our intentions. We remember the embarrassment of facing our friends and families when things didn't work out as we had expected. We remember the pain of quitting when everything seemed hopeless.

Second, we try to predict the future. In our fortune telling way of living, we try to predict the outcome of our efforts before it happens. We look to the future and try to predict or determine everywhere we might fail before we begin. We try to determine every potential problem that might arise and stop our progress. As a result, we focus on the problems—not the solutions—and convince ourselves that no matter how much we want to do something, the problems are too large, or there are too many problems to overcome. Because of our lack of confidence in ourselves, we accept defeat.

Third, we allow others to talk us out of trying. We listen to others as they tell us we are wasting our time. We listen to them as they make fun of and laugh at our ideas. We take everything they say to heart and over time begin to believe what they are saying.

Fourth, we convince ourselves that we are under qualified. We tell ourselves that we need some type of special education, title, or status in the community to succeed at our dreams. We rationalize that, because we are not the special person we think we ought to be, we are not up to the task at hand and can never be successful.

The last thing that keeps us from trying is our ability to plan. That's right, our ability to plan. Most seminars and books about achieving success preach the benefits of spending quality time planning. They suggest we set goals and go through a defined sequence of events before starting. They encourage us to spend significant amounts of time filling out goal sheets, breaking every task into a hundred little steps, and mapping out what we should do and when we should do it. Frankly, while it sounds like a good idea, it doesn't always work. Most people get so involved in planning and filling out their goal sheets that they get bogged down in the process and lose sight of their ultimate goals.

Two things happen when we over plan. One, we talk ourselves out of trying when we realize and identify all the tasks and problems ahead of us. It's scary when, in the process of filling out goal sheets, we begin to see all the obstacles in front of us that we must overcome. We begin to doubt ourselves. We start to question our abilities to meet the challenges. Our fears of failing talk us out of trying something before we begin.

Two, we spend precious time planning that we could spend doing. Every problem we run into and every deadline we miss throws our goal sheets into tailspins. Our sheets are no longer accurate, and we have to revise or redo them altogether. It's not that filling out goal sheets is difficult, but the time we spend filling out, correcting, and redoing the sheets every time we encounter a problem or a new idea bores us with the process and we lose interest. Tracking and filling out goal sheets is tedious work that takes us away from time that could be spent doing. We over plan, we over prepare, we over chart our course, we get frustrated, and as a result, we never do. We never get started. We can plan all we want, but if we are not doing something to live our dreams every day, we are not going to succeed.

Some planning and goal setting is good. Some planning and goal setting is necessary. However, planning and goal setting will not make you successful without action. In fact, the opposite can be true. Spending excessive amounts of time planning and not living your dream will keep you from being successful. Think about it, how can you be successful if you are spending all of your quality time planning? By doing this, no matter how hard you try, you will never have enough time to follow your dream. To be successful, you must spend quality time acting on your dream.

How much planning is too much? Only you can answer that question for yourself, but here are a few signs that should alert you to a problem. If you find yourself spending more time filling out goal sheets than working toward your dream, you're probably spending too much time planning. If you are worrying about breaking each task into a hundred individual steps, you're probably spending too much time planning. If you can't start a task without writing it down on a goal sheet, you're probably spending too much time planning. If your goal is to have every step of the journey planned in detail, with a solution to every conceivable problem imaginable, you're probably spending too much time planning. If planning is keeping you from accomplishing your dream, you are without a doubt spending too much time planning. Any one of these could keep you from becoming successful. Only do what planning is necessary to get you started and to keep you on track moving forward.

If you want to succeed, approach every opportunity like a child. Children are doers. They learn and are successful by doing. They take their dreams and ideas and, with very little reflection, run with them. They don't allow memories of past failures keep them from trying. Children rarely give up at the first sign of failure. My children seemed to know instinctively that what happened in the past is rarely an indicator for what will happen in the future.

Children don't try to predict the future, but live only for today. To children, today is the future. They don't worry about potential problems that might arise. They don't let real or imaginary problems bother them. If something doesn't work as they think it should, they try something else. Children will rarely let a problem distract them, slow them down, or stop them from doing something they want to do.

Children don't let other people talk them out of trying their ideas or going after their dreams. They don't care what other people think. They don't care what other people say. They don't let anyone discourage them from doing what is important to them or keep them from being successful.

Children could care less if they are qualified to do something when it comes to doing something they want to do. Education, title, or status means nothing to them. All that matters to them is their determination to accomplish what they set out to accomplish.

Children don't over plan. In fact, they do very little planning. Children don't even know what a goal sheet is or how to fill one out. If something doesn't go as they had planned, they make a new plan and change direction without a second thought.

Have you ever heard of the scientific method? Sure you have! We all learned about it in science class in high school. It is a process to look at problems and test theories using a structured sequence of steps. In business, people call it many different things like Six Sigma, Total Quality Management, and Zero Defects. If you haven't heard of these, I'm sure you will very soon. Using the scientific method you state the problem, establish a theory on what needs to be done to correct it, test the theory, check to see if what you did worked and if it worked, you make the changes permanent; otherwise, you come up with something else to try, and start the process over again. Of course, with Six Sigma you make it a lot harder than it really is by using a lot of statistical analysis to prove to yourself and the world that what you are doing is right, but this process is nothing new. No matter what the name or analysis method, it is the same process you used as a child. It wasn't until we were in high school or later in life that we attached a fancy name to what we had been doing all along. It was what Jonathan used to fix his walkie-talkie, and it is what all children use to overcome challenges they face as they mature.

In Jonathan's case, he wanted to fix his walkie-talkie. That was the most important thing in his life at that moment. First, he came up with an idea of what he thought might fix it. Second, he tried it. Third, he checked to see if what he tried worked by turning on his walkie-talkie. Finally, if what he tried didn't work, he thought of something else that might work and started the process over again. Once he determined what would fix it, he made the fix permanent and the rest is history.

Jonathan never worried about failing. He never even considered it. He had confidence in himself that he was going to be successful no matter what happened or how long it took.

Jonathan didn't allow the memories of past failures or the problems he encountered slow him down. Can you imagine the problems he confronted while he tried to fix his walkie-talkie? The different things he must have tried that didn't work? It's mind-boggling! Did he let his disappointments get him down when what he tried didn't work? No, he just tried something else.

Jonathan didn't try to predict the future. He didn't try to predict where he might fail before he started. He didn't try to determine every problem before it came up. He never focused on the problems; he only focused on the solutions.

Jonathan didn't let anyone talk him out of trying. Neither my wife nor I could discourage him from attempting to fix his walkie-talkie. He heard us talking about him in the kitchen. He heard us having a good laugh at his expense, but he didn't care what we thought or what we said. He knew in his heart he could fix his radio if he kept trying.

Jonathan never considered the fact that people would not consider him qualified to fix his radio. It didn't matter to him that he didn't have a degree in electronics from a reputable school. It didn't matter to him that he didn't know the first thing about walkie-talkies. I'm sure he told himself repeatedly that if he kept working on his radio that eventually he would fix it.

Jonathan didn't allow planning to get in his way of doing. He only did what planning was necessary. He didn't fill out goal sheets before he started. He didn't break down every task into a hundred separate goals. Jonathan made mental notes of things he could try as he worked. He recalled other things he had tried while fixing other toys. Jonathan only did what planning was necessary to accomplish his goal. What planning was done was done while fixing his walkie-talkie.

Jonathan stayed focused. He didn't let the distractions around him take him away from his goal. He didn't play with his friends in the neighborhood. He didn't watch his favorite television shows with his family. If fact, Jonathan was so focused on fixing his toy, he didn't even want to stop to eat. How many times have we skipped a meal to pursue our dreams?

Children make time to do what is important to them. Even over the best intentions of a parent, they rarely let anything stop them from doing something they really want to do. If children are determined to do something, they are going to do it. Their dreams of what they want to do or who they want to be control their thoughts and drive them to action, which in turn, leads them to success.

How did Jonathan fix his radio? He didn't know anything about electronics. He didn't even understand how the radio worked. He took the radio that worked and compared it against the radio that didn't. As he put the radios back together, he noticed a wire on the broken radio that had come loose. Once he reconnected the wire, it started working. It was as simple as that. Would an adult have even tried to fix it?

We have often heard that how we spend our time indicates what is important to us. What's important to you? How do you spend your time? Are you spending your time on the things that are most important to you? Or are you spending your time on things that are not taking you in the direction you want to go? If you are not spending your time on the things that are most important to you, what is keeping you from doing it?

Growing up in the Colbert-Lauderdale counties of Northwest Alabama provided access to some of the most beautiful waterways in America. As I have traveled across the country, few compare. Because of the many natural resources available, fishing is a major recreational activity. Fishermen come from all over the world to fish there.

While I was home visiting family a few months ago, I was told a story about a fisherman who came to visit the area. He stopped in a little store on the side of the road to ask about a small lake he had noticed on his way into town.

"How's the fishing at the lake back down the road?" he asked.

"It yoosta—that's how they say it in Alabama—to be real good until about three years ago. Then the hole just dried up," the storeowner said as the helped another customer. "Ain't nobody caught nothin' in that hole in years."

"Do you think anybody would mind if I give it a try?" asked the fisherman.

"Not at all, but I'm telling you, you're wasting your time," said the storeowner as the fisherman left the store.

Later that afternoon the fisherman returned to the store with buckets of fish. The storeowner and his customers were shocked to see all the fish he had caught. It was the talk of the store for the rest of the afternoon.

The next afternoon the fisherman returned with even more buckets of fish. Just like yesterday, the storeowner and his customers were amazed at the number of fish the man had caught.

"We don't understand how you're catchin' all them fish," said the storeowner. "Ain't nobody caught nothin' out of that hole in over three years. We've had some of the best fishermen in these parts try that hole, and they didn't catch a thing. We just figured there weren't any more fish in that fishin' hole."

On this day, the local game warden just happened to be in the store on his day off and overheard their conversation. He, too, was amazed. In fact, he was so amazed that he wanted to see it for himself. "Can I come fishin' with you tomorrow and see how you are catchin' all them fish?" he asked.

"Sure!" said the fisherman. "There are plenty of fish for everyone."

Early the next day, the fisherman and the game warden set out in the fisherman's boat. The game warden was especially talkative about the great plans they made to restock the lake a couple of years ago, but nothing came of it. "You know how politicians are!" said the game warden. "They will promise you anything to get your vote!"

As soon as they had reached the middle of the lake, the fisherman reached down into a duffel bag sitting by his feet and pulled out a stick of dynamite. In one quick motion, the fisherman lit the dynamite and threw it into the water.

Ca - Booooooom!

Within a matter of seconds, fish began to float to the top of the water. The fisherman reached down into the water with his net and began to pull the fish into the boat.

The game warden was infuriated. He stood up in the boat and began to shout, "You can't do that! That's against the law!"

The fisherman, without saying a word, carefully reached down into the same duffel bag. In one motion he pulled out another stick of dynamite and lit it. Without pause, he handed it to the game warden. As the fisherman leaned back, he said, "Are you going to fish, or are you going to talk all day?"

Now don't take this silly story the wrong way. I'm not suggesting you break the law—far from it. By telling this story, I'm only suggesting that sometimes when we start out with a goal in mind we get so caught up thinking, planning, and trying to anticipate every possible problem that we never get started. We dwell on our failures—past and future—without considering the possibility of success. Instead of going after our dreams, we end up just talking about what we are going to do some day. For most of us, that day never comes.

In this story the people of the little community hadn't even tried the fishing hole in three years. Because of memories of past fishing trips and thoughts of possible future failures, they assumed there were no fish in the lake and didn't go there to fish anymore. Not only had they talked each other out of trying the lake for the past three years, but they tried to talk the fisherman out of trying as well. They assumed that because some of the best fishermen in the area—who they considered more qualified than themselves—didn't catch anything, neither could they. They made plans to restock the lake, but after encountering an obstacle, gave up the idea and never acted on it. In the end, they convinced themselves that they would be wasting their time going there to fish.

In contrast to the thoughts of the little town, the fisherman showed them in just a few minutes there were fish in the lake for the taking for those who would try. Please don't misunderstand. You should never fish with dynamite; it will get you arrested! But because of the extreme measures the fisherman took, he showed the little community that there were fish to catch. The story illustrates that there were fish in the lake, but because of past experiences and a myriad of other reasons, nobody even tried to catch them.

Don't get caught up in the memories of the past or the possibilities of failure in the future. Clear your mind of past failures. What happened in the past is never an indicator of what will happen in the future. Failure has always been and always will be a prerequisite of success. Rarely, throughout the history of mankind, has there been any worthwhile developed idea, product, or invention that didn't go through a period of failure.

Failure is going to happen. Any time you are trying new things, testing new ideas, or going into uncharted waters, failure is bound to happen.

Correct your mistakes, forget your failures, and move forward toward your goal. Never let memories of past failures or possible future failures keep you from trying.

Don't let other people talk you out of doing something you want to do. Only you know what will make you happy. If there is something you want to do, then do it. Disregard what others say. In the end, you will only have to answer to yourself, not to them.

Don't let not being qualified stop you from trying. Success has never depended on whether a person is qualified or not. Success has never depended on education, title, or status. Some of the most successful people in the world have never had any of these things. Take Dave Thomas of the Wendy's Hamburger chain. Here is a man that developed and built a company into one of the most successful fast food restaurants in the world. I doubt that anyone would have considered him qualified when he started. He didn't have a special title or community status. He didn't have advanced degrees in management or corporate finance. In fact, it wasn't until after his business was a huge success that he earned his GED and received a high school diploma.

Success doesn't depend on your level of education. Success doesn't depend on whether you are the boss or a part-time employee of your company. Success doesn't depend on whether you are the mayor or an average citizen of your community. Success depends on you. If you choose to be successful, you can and will be.

Don't let planning get in the way of doing what you need to do. Never spend your quality time planning. Spend your quality time doing. Don't allow yourself to get so bogged down in planning and trying to predict the future that you never make time to work on your dream. Planning will not make you successful. Success only comes by doing.

I truly believe that those who "do and then think" are often more successful than those who "think and then do." The thinkers never quit thinking and may never move into action. They constantly think about all the reasons that could cause them to fail. They never stop planning and plan themselves right out of doing. They always have some reason, whether real or imaginary, that keeps them from getting started.

Be like a child. Remember when you were a child? Be a doer and get started. Make a commitment right now to do something that will move you toward your dream. Even if you go east to get west, do it now! Even if it is not the shortest route to where you are going, you are at least moving toward your ultimate destination. Take each step with courage. The first step of any journey is always the hardest.

Commit yourself to living your dreams. How can you expect to realize your dreams if you never act on them? You probably won't have your dreams handed to you on a platter. Make your dreams come alive, not in your mind, but through your actions. Work hard, sacrifice, and focus your energies on achieving your dreams. Make your "someday" today, and live out your dreams in your daily life. Success comes to those who look to the heavens, see the stars among the clouds, and reach for them.

Commit Yourself

To be successful at anything, as simple as this may sound, you must commit yourself to being successful. You must make your goal or dream one of the top priorities in your life. It doesn't matter what you are trying to accomplish, you must dedicate the time and effort needed to be successful. If you are not willing to make the commitment necessary to accomplish your goal or dream, most likely you will not reach your full potential or realize your objective as you envisioned it.

What do I mean by being committed? You have gotta want it bad! You can't just be a casual participant. You must commit your heart and soul to the task and make it one of the most important things in your life.

Just like a finely tuned athlete, you must make the time to do what it takes to be successful. Does a gold medalist in the Olympics spend a few days a year getting ready for his or her competition? No, they spend almost every waking hour training and working on improving their performance. They work out for hours a day—every day—for years to perfect their athletic ability to rise to top-tier within their sport. To be successful at anything, so must you. Commitment is the first fundamental element of being successful at everything you do and is the first building block of success.

If we have dreams and think we know what we want to accomplish, why do we have trouble committing the time necessary to achieve our goals?

Five things get in the way of us fully committing to our goals or dreams: having a false dream, lack of confidence, having the wrong attitude, allowing others to create roadblocks in our path, and the word 'no'. Let's look at each one and see how they affect each of us.

The first thing that keeps us from fully committing to whatever we want to accomplish is what I call a false dream. In other words, we think we want something, but as soon as we think about doing the things that are necessary to accomplishing our dream, we never take the first step. We never allow the idea in our mind to take a step of action towards our goal. If we never act on an idea or a goal, it is a false dream. Oh, we may say it is a dream we want to accomplish, but it really isn't a dream at all. It is only a passing thought that we are spending too much time on. If it were something we really wanted to achieve and we were fully committed to doing it, we wouldn't hesitate to start doing the things that are necessary to accomplish our goal.

A good example of a false dream is sometimes related to a personal habit. Someone who claims he or she wants to quit smoking, but never does falls into this category. I have known many smokers throughout my lifetime that claim they really want and need to quit smoking, but they never do. Why? Because, like they tell me, they enjoy smoking. They know they need to quit because of the health ramifications it sometimes causes, but they like to smoke. It gives them pleasure and fills a need in their lives.

Losing weight is another good example of a false dream. How many times have we all said that we need to lose a few pounds? We all know we need to, but we don't. Why? Because food gives us comfort. It makes us happy! We know we need to give up our extra serving of mashed potatoes, but it really tastes good! Because of our inability to stop eating, a multi-billion-dollar industry thrives on our false hopes of achieving a goal that we never truly commit to. As a result, we are a country full of overweight people living to eat, not eating to live. To be successful at anything, your goal or dream must be treated as a prerequisite to your happiness, and you must commit to it becoming a top priority in your life.

The second thing that keeps us from committing to whatever we want to accomplish is our lack of confidence. We spend a lot more time on this later, but self-confidence is an essential fundamental element in being successful at anything. If you want to accomplish something, you must believe without reservation that you can.

Third with self-confidence comes the need to have the right attitude. Not having the right attitude will make it difficult if not impossible to commit to anything. Having the right attitude is essential to being successful. Here again we spend more time on the right attitude later in the book, but suffice it to say at this point that having the right attitude is another fundamental element of being successful and gives you the stick-to-itiveness necessary to make you successful at everything you do.

Not only must we believe in our self and have the right attitude, fourth, we must not allow others to erect roadblocks in front of us. Allowing others to create doubt, fear of failure, or hopelessness in our mind keeps us from committing to what we want to achieve.

How does the seeding of doubt in our mind happen? It happens because of our lack of confidence, the insecurities of the people that we share our life with, and the lack of confidence these people have within themselves. These people, for whatever reason, are not accomplishing their dreams, so to make themselves feel better they subconsciously and sometimes consciously create doubts in our head to confuse our commitment to our dream.

Why do people do this? In reality, these kinds of people don't want us to accomplish our goals, and as silly as this may sound, they think it makes them look bad if we are successful. In their minds, preventing us from accomplishing our dreams by creating doubts in us makes them feel better about not accomplishing their own goals. To be successful at anything, we must force these people out of our lives, and if necessary, get restraining orders to keep them away from us. Never allow these people to stop you from chasing your dreams.

The final thing that keeps us from fully committing to whatever we want to accomplish is the word 'no'. No is the most potentially destructive word in any language. It has destroyed hopes, dreams, and opportunities for thousands of years. It has prevented ideas from being considered and developed. It has ruined brilliant careers and organizations of all sizes. It has shattered friendships, relationships and partnerships. People have used it in conjunction with almost every excuse ever offered. It is rarely associated with anything positive and is a huge hindrance to success. Because this word is so powerful, I want to spend a little more time on this commitment breaker.

How many times has one of us gone to someone with an idea, and their first reaction to us was a no. They didn't even allow us to finish our thought before they gave us their answer. They said something like, "That will never work," or "That's the craziest thing I have ever heard." Without thought, without discussion, they kill our idea and dash our dream.

How does it make you feel when someone tells you no without listening? Do you get upset when they shoot down your idea before allowing you to present it? Do you think they treated you unfairly? Did he or she make it seem like your idea had no value? Did it make you want to come back and offer another idea at a later date? Probably not. I mean, who wants to be rejected without even being heard?

Not only does this happen to us, but we do the same thing to other people. How many times has someone come to us with an idea, and we told him or her no without explanation? We didn't allow that person to expand on or explain his or her thought before we tossed it aside. Were we so busy that we didn't have time to listen to the possibilities? Did a distraction cause us to react this way? Did we close our minds because we were angry with the person or something else unrelated to this event? What caused us to respond this way?

Adults can be disrespectful to each other on occasion. Sometimes I think it is part of our DNA makeup to be hurtful to other adults. Instead of taking the time to hear someone's idea and give a reasonable constructive response, we hide behind the word no and refuse to even consider the possibilities of the idea.

However, adults are not only disrespectful to each other; we treat our children the same way. Our children come to us with things they want to do, and we say "no" before they can finish asking. They try to tell us something that happened at school, and we tell them to be quiet so we can hear the television. They ask us a question, and we respond with "not right now." We treat them just like others treat us. We respond to them with the easiest answer that requires no thought or action—"no."

But children are different in the way they respond to the word no. Unlike adults who, at the first encounter of hearing the word no, kill their ideas and stop pursuing their goals and dreams, children will not take no for an answer. If they think their ideas are reasonable, they will reject our answers, and our responses become their motivation to do whatever it takes to get the results they want. They are fully committed to their ideas in spite of our negative responses. In fact, children will pretend to not even understand the concept of the word and are prepared to stand toe-to-toe with us to get what they want. They act as if the word no doesn't even exist in their vocabulary.

Adults can learn a lot from remembering how children respond to the word no. Basically, children use three methods to get around the word no. First, they will use other people, like your spouse, to their advantage. I call it *The Equal Authority Slide*. For example, my daughter Kristen comes to me asking to spend the night with a friend. Before she can finish asking, I tell her "no." Does this stop Kristen? Of course not, she slides right past me like I wasn't even there. She immediately goes to my wife and asks her the same question. She may change her approach a little to assure a more favorable response, but she disregards my answer completely. After some discussion, my wife agrees with my daughter and says it's okay. The next thing I know, Kristen is leaving to go over to her friend's house to spend the night. In this case, Kristen used the other authority figure of our household—my wife—to attain the result or answer she was looking for. It's sneaky, but effective.

The second method involves people outside the family unit. I call it *The Outsiders Shuffle*. Using the same example, Kristen comes to me and asks to spend the night with one of her friends. Here again, I say "no." This time she doesn't go to my wife, but instead goes to someone outside the family for support. In this particular case, Kristen approaches the mother of the friend that she wants to spend the night with and gets her involved. Kristen elicits her support and gets her to ask my wife and me if it would be all right for her to sleep over. After a short discussion and time of begging, we reluctantly agree to let her spend the night. In this case, Kristen uses an authority figure outside our household to gain support and sway the decision of her own authority figures. This method is most often used when the child determines that the first method will not work.

The final method is perhaps the most daring of all. They don't even ask. They just do it. I call it *The in Your Face* method. With this method, they decided that method one and two will not work and proceed to do what they wanted to do without asking. They've determined that in this situation, the potential benefit that will result from this action far outweighs the risk involved in getting caught disobeying. Children are naturally risk takers and have a sixth sense about knowing what they should and shouldn't tell their parents. Kristen has a keen sixth sense. Just like most children, she knows when to ask or tell and when to keep quiet.

When Kristen was younger, she had beautiful, long blonde hair. She didn't take care of it like my wife and I would have liked her to, but when it was combed and styled, it was gorgeous. When she didn't comb it, she wore a Daffy Duck baseball hat. My wife and I threatened to cut her hair on occasion when we were having trouble getting her to take care of it. But that never happened. She would never let anyone cut her hair.

Kristen likes to chew gum more than anyone I know. From the time she got up in the morning until she went to bed at night, she had gum in her mouth. She liked to stretch the gum and play with it more than anything. She would hold one end of the gum between her teeth while she pulled the other end out of her mouth with her thumb and first finger. Kristen stretched it out as far as her arm could reach, and then she would bite it back into her mouth. If we told her one time, we told her a thousand times to stop playing with her gum. Did Kristen ever listen? No. Playing with her gum was important to her, and she felt that we were being unreasonable and would ignore our pleas for her to stop. Kristen lost her gum regularly because of her actions.

Sometimes she would sneak gum into her bed at night after all the lights were out. I can see her in my mind now—lying on her back in bed, stretching her gum, and having the time of her life knowing that she wasn't supposed to be doing it. Just before she would fall to sleep, she would take the gum out of her mouth and put it on a scrap of paper sitting on the table next to her bed. At least, that is what she normally did.

However, one night Kristen fell asleep before she could remove her gum. To her surprise, the next morning when she woke up, she had gum stuck down the side of her face and in her hair. She had obviously fallen asleep in the middle of a pull before she could bite it back into her mouth. Did Kristen jump out of bed, run into our room, and tell us what she did? No. Did she run to the neighbor's house and ask for help? No. Did she go to her brother's room, wake him up, and ask him what to do? No. He would tell on her. Kristen did the only thing she could do. She sneaked into the bathroom, locked the door, washed her face, and cut the gum out of her hair. Kristen did this so covertly, that my wife and I didn't find out about it until years later.

Kristen used *The in Your Face* method to do something that was important to her in spite of our constant rejection of the idea. She knew if she asked to chew gum in her bed, we would say no. She knew that asking for support from other people would be a waste of time. She weighed the risk and decided to go forward. When she woke up with gum in her hair, she dealt with the problem without our knowledge and continued to chew gum in her bed. Of course, she learned from her mistake to always remove her gum before she fell asleep, and as a result, to my knowledge she never got gum in her hair again. Only after Kristen accidentally blurted the incident out years later did my wife and I even know. By then it didn't matter.

Do you remember using these same three tactics to get your way when you were a child? Sure you do. We've all used them. As simple as these examples may seem, adults can still employ the three methods Kristen used to get around the word no.

If you believe in your idea, you must never accept no for an answer. You must use whatever methods are necessary to get your idea accepted and moving into action. If possible, just as you did as a child, you should try to eliminate the word no from your vocabulary. Does this mean that you lie, cheat, or steal to get your way? No, of course not! Do you deceive others to gain support for your ideas? No, you push forward, always doing what is right, never allowing anyone who could keep you from being successful stand in your way. A child wouldn't let it happen, and neither should you.

To further illustrate these concepts, let's say you have a money-saving idea that you have been thinking about for a while. You have a new process that, if implemented, could save your company a huge amount of money. You go to your boss and begin to tell him or her about your idea. For whatever reason, he or she says "no." However, you still believe you have a valuable idea. Do you accept their answer and forget about it? If you truly believe in your idea, you can never take no for an answer. So, what do you do? You talk to everyone in your organization you think will support your idea. You go to your boss' peers, your peers, or anyone else who could influence the decision. You present your idea and elicit support.

In addition to going to directly to your peers, you go to people in your company who will benefit from your idea, and get them onboard. You talk to people who will reap the savings as a result of your idea. It could be time-savings, manpower savings, or any other kind of savings. Anyone who could benefit from your idea is a potential supporter of your cause.

Once you have enough support, call a meeting with all those involved, and present your idea again. Be sure to invite your boss to the meeting. During the meeting, allow those in support of you to help explain the benefits they will reap from your idea. Hopefully, your boss or the decision maker will be overwhelmed by the support for your idea and will agree to let it go forward.

Here we used *The Equal Authority Slide* to gain acceptance of our idea and accomplish our goal. When we didn't receive the answer we expected or wanted from our boss, we solicited support from other people of authority in the organization. Once our boss saw the unified front and understood how our idea would benefit others in the organization, he gave in, accepted our idea, and let it move forward into action. Just as the method indicates, we slid by the individual or individuals blocking our idea and gathered support from the other authority figures within our organization to gain acceptance.

The second method—*The Outsiders Shuffle*—is a little different. For example, let's say you have a new method of doing business that departs from the way your company has traditionally operated. You think your idea is good, but because of your concern that it doesn't fit the traditional mold, you're convinced you will need additional help to sell your idea.

So how do you sell an idea that will transform your company? You talk with your customers. You find out what they think about your idea and solicit their support. You talk to other noncompeting companies that have done or tried similar things. You talk to consultants and vendors in your industry, and use their experience and resources to support your cause. Bottom-line, you talk to anyone outside of your company who could help sell your idea, and get their feedback and buy in. In the end, you present your idea to everyone that could possibly have skin in the game, and ask them if they are interested in your new approach. If they say yes, you ask them for their support.

Once you think you have enough support for your idea, approach the leadership of your company. Present your idea, and show them the support you have garnered from the people outside of your company for your new way of doing business. Your company's leadership will be hard-pressed to say no to your idea when you show them all the support you have attracted from others outside the company.

I have a friend who used *The Outsiders Shuffle* to start a business. His name is Ron Camp. Ron wanted to start a telecommunications business. He had many years of experience in the industry and was tired of working for someone else. He had a good business idea, a good marketing plan, and hundreds of contacts throughout the country. Regrettably, there was one thing Ron didn't have. He didn't have start-up money or capital required to get his business up and running.

Every bank that Ron presented his business plan to turned him down. Each one gave him a lot of financial mumbo-jumbo and told him he didn't qualify for a business loan. Did Ron give up? No. He used *The Outsiders Shuffle.*

He started calling his contacts. He told them about his plans and asked for their feedback and support. Within two weeks, Ron secured seven contracts that would more than secure the money he was asking to borrow. Ron went back to the bank, presented his idea and business plan to them again, handed them the letters from companies intending to do business with him once he was up and running, and guess what? He secured the loan he needed to start his business. Thanks to *The Outsiders Shuffle*, Ron is now a successful businessman doing what he used to only dream about doing.

Unfortunately, *The Equal Authority Slide* and *The Outsiders Shuffle* are not always appropriate in every situation. Sometimes you can't ask for help from others. Sometimes you have to take a chance and take the risk yourself. Granted, most use this method as a last resort, but sometimes you don't have any other course of action if you believe in your idea and are committed to seeing it through. Sometimes you have to use *The in Your Face* method, and just do it! You have to go out on your own, take a giant leap of faith, and do whatever you are going to do without authority or approval. However, when using this method, you must be totally committed to your idea, and conclude that the realized benefit of your actions will be much greater than the risk involved in trying. As it has been said many times before, sometimes it is easier to ask for forgiveness than to ask for permission.

What ideas do you have that, up until now, have not been given an opportunity to develop? Is there someone in your life who blocks you every step of the way? What is keeping your ideas from growing and preventing you from being successful? Just like it was when you were a child, you should never take no for an answer. You should never let anyone block you or keep you from developing a great idea or pursuing your dreams. Use the methods that we all used as children, and turn the word no into yes.

Unlike the word no, yes is the most powerful word in the universe. It allows ideas to develop and opportunities to flourish. It diffuses problems before they can begin to develop. It allows imaginations to thrive and dreams to prosper.

The next time someone says no to you, smile, say yes to yourself, and attack the rejection as you did when you were a child. A child rarely takes no for an answer, and neither should you.

So, what did we learn? To be successful at anything, we must be totally committed to our goals and dreams. We have to make our ideas a top priority in our lives. How do we become committed? First, we reject false dreams and quit spending our time thinking about ideas that we never intend to develop or act on. This only distracts us from our real dreams and keeps us from moving into action on the things that are really important to us. Second, we believe in ourselves, knowing we can accomplish anything we commit to. Having doubts about our own abilities only hinders or delays our possibilities for success. Third, we pursue our idea with the right attitude that gives us the stick-to-itiveness needed to stay on track and complete our goals. We don't give up at the first sign of trouble, but we stay focused on our goals and move them to completion. Fourth, we must never permit anyone to place roadblocks in our path or allow them to suggest to us that our ideas are not legitimate by creating doubt within our mind about our dreams. If there are people in our lives who are constantly degrading our ideas, we must distance ourselves from them as quickly as possible. Finally, using the same methods we used as children, we must try to eliminate the word no from our vocabulary, and turn the rejection we sometimes encounter into acceptance. If we believe in our ideas, we must never let the word no discourage us from chasing our dreams.

If you want to be successful at everything you do, fully commit yourself to your idea or dream, and move it from the someday part of your mind to a priority in your life. You must move your dream from inactivity into action. Being committed to your dream is the first fundamental element of success. Commit to your dream and live it.

Believe In Yourself

To be successful, we must believe in ourselves. We must have the utmost confidence in our abilities that we can do anything we put our minds to. Just as our commitments are vital to our successes, so is confidence and the belief that we can accomplish everything we commit to. Believing in ourselves is the second fundamental element of the building blocks of success.

How is your confidence? Do you want to be successful? Are you willing to develop the right attitude to stay committed to whatever you want to accomplish? Are you willing to adapt to changes needed to complete a task? Do you think you are as smart as anyone else is? Are you willing to learn new skills if necessary? Are you willing to work as hard as it takes? Can you work with other people to complete a task or to achieve a goal? If you answered yes to these questions, then why wouldn't you have confidence in your abilities to be successful? You just answered yes to all the questions that represent the fundamental elements of being successful.

I assure you that, for you to get to this point in your life, you have had many successes. Some are big and have memorial tokens that hang on a wall or are in a scrapbook. Some are smaller that may not even invoke a memory now but were special at that moment. Others were insignificant and not even recognized at the time but were successes just the same. However grandiose or insignificant your successes were to get you to where you are now, you've had thousands, if not millions, of successes along the way that have become part of your life's history. Just based on this history alone, you should be confident that you can do anything you want to do; anything you commit to.

From the moment of birth, parents start convincing their children they can do almost anything. Within minutes after babies breathe their first breaths of air, parents begin to bombard their children with words of encouragement in their best baby voices. "You're such a pretty baby!" "You're the prettiest baby in the whole world!" "You're going to be president someday!" "You're so smart!" "You're going to get a scholarship to one of the best schools in the country!" "You're going to grow up and do or be anything you want to be," we say.

Every time their children accomplish something—no matter how large or small—they congratulate them and tell everyone how wonderful they are. "Good Job!" "What a good baby!" "That was great!" "Did you see my baby do that?" they ask. Every parent acts as if this was the first time any baby, anywhere on the planet, has ever done this particular thing. Children make their parents proud, and they express their pride to anyone who will listen.

Because of this pride, sometimes parents turn their children into circus performers as they practice their new learned skills. Parents make friends watch while their babies repeat new skills over and over. Parents stop complete strangers, wherever they may be at the time, seize their attention, and coerce them into watching their children perform. Parents are proud of their children and show them off every chance they get. You may not remember it now, but your parents were probably the same way with you.

My wife and I were no different with our children. I can remember when my son Jonathan began to walk. We met every stage of his development with excitement. Every new accomplishment was treated as if it was his first. His achievements brought joy to my wife and I, and we spoke our assuring words to Jonathan every step of the way. And yes, we showed him off to everyone every chance we got.

Before Jonathan could crawl, we used to lay him on his stomach on a pallet in the middle of the floor. We strategically placed his favorite toys all around him within his line of sight but just outside his reach. As soon as the first toy was in place, the strangest thing would happen. He would raise his arms and legs up off the floor and try to scoot himself forward on his tummy. He looked like a skydiver flying through the air as he tried to move closer to his toy. As always, our words affirmed him as he worked to move forward.

A short time later, Jonathan lowered his arms and began to drag himself. He used his hands, arms, and elbows like a soldier in battle to move himself forward while he dragged his body and legs behind him. Although this was a vast improvement over his previous method, it still didn't get him anywhere fast, but it got him where he wanted to go, and we congratulated him every time he did it.

It wasn't long before Jonathan learned how to sit up. I was in Pine Bluff, Arkansas, on an extended business trip at the time and heard about it over the phone. This was one of the saddest days of my life. Not because Jonathan learned how to do something that would move him a step closer to walking, but because I was so far away and couldn't be there to experience his accomplishment and share in the excitement of the moment. It just about killed me—my first born learning to sit up while I sat in a motel room several hundred miles away, not knowing when I would be returning home.

As we talked each night on the phone, I made my wife describe to me over the next several days how Jonathan sat up. I made her repeat the story nightly. No detail was too small to leave out. A mental picture formed in my mind as she described his every action. I could feel my wife's excitement of the experience as I checked on his progress.

This same excitement kept me going throughout the next day as I recounted the conversations to my coworkers. I told them everything about Jonathan. I didn't leave out any detail. I replayed my mental picture of Jonathan sitting up to anyone who would listen. I'm sure that some of them got tired of hearing about it, and others tried to avoid me, but I was proud of my son and missed being there with him to share in his moment.

Within no time, Jonathan was up on his hands and knees. He didn't know what to do when he got there and demonstrated his uncertainly as he rocked back and forth, never moving his hands or knees. As he swayed back and forth, his movement got larger and larger until he finally lost his balance and fell forward on his face. I'm sure it hurt, but he didn't seem to mind. He whined a little, got back up on his hands and knees, and rocked back and forth until he fell on his face again. Every time he fell on his face, he moved forward about six inches. Our friends and neighbors watched with amazement as he repeated this action over and over. He wasn't crawling yet, but it was another success story in his progression to walk.

About this same time, we bought Jonathan a walker. You know, one of those gizmos with wheels you sit your baby in that allows his feet to touch the floor to simulate walking. It had three or four wheels along the base that allows it to roll in any direction. Jonathan loved it! He no longer had to scrape his stomach or skin his nose to get to where he wanted to go. He could sit upright and use his feet to move himself around the room. Of course, there was one problem. He never went forward. Everywhere he went he looked over his right shoulder as if he were backing the family car out of the garage.

We tried everything to make Jonathan go forward. We tried standing in front of him and calling him toward us. We tried moving his toys so that they were always in front of him before he started. We tried backing him into a corner until he couldn't move, thinking it would force him to go forward, but nothing ever worked. He was determined to go backward. It didn't matter what we did. He just whipped around and pushed himself backward with his feet as fast as he could.

One night while I bounced him on my knees, he grabbed my index fingers with both of his hands and stood up straight. From that moment forward, with his feet firmly planted on my legs and one of my fingers in each of his hands, he never sat down again. He stood as tall as he could, his head turning from side to side to survey the room. He loved standing on my legs holding my fingers and would spend hours at a time doing it. I was happy for him to do it and displayed him standing on my knees to everyone who passed through our home.

Once Jonathan stood up, it wasn't long before he was walking. He pushed aside the ways of an infant, moved into the toddler stage, and began to walk everywhere he went. He refused to let anyone carry him. He refused to let anyone push him in his stroller. Jonathan was proud of the new skill he had achieved as much as my wife and I were, and he showed it off to everyone. Because of Jonathan's determination and commitment to walk, he walked everywhere he wanted to go.

In addition to parents encouraging their children to show off their skills as performers, they sometimes unknowingly encourage them to go out on a limb and attempt things they may not be physically or mentally ready to try. Parents want their child to be the best and greatest at everything they do. They want them to be smarter than any other child is. They want them to do things sooner than any other child has ever done things before. Parents want their children to stand above all other children, and as a result, they sometimes push them into trying things that they may not be capable of doing. They convince their children to take chances by saying things like: "You can do it!" "It's easy!" "Don't be afraid!" "Just try one time for Daddy!" "Daddy would never let you do anything that he didn't think you were ready to do!" "I know you can do it!" And when their children try and fail, parents never get mad or discouraged, but encourage their children to try again.

When my daughter Kristen began to show signs of walking, my wife and I pushed her to the limit. Even though it was early for most children her age to walk, because of her excitement around the subject and her eagerness to try, we were sure she was ready to walk and willing to accept our assistance. So we did what every parent does; we pushed her a little harder. We stood her up so that she could place one hand on the couch to steady herself. We backed up two or three baby steps, out stretched our hands, and shouted words of encouragement. "Come on Kristen, you can do it!" "Momma and Daddy know you can do it!" "There is nothing to it!" "Move your feet, and come to Momma!" "We know you can do it!" But Kristen never moved. She just stood there and smiled at us with all three of her teeth.

With her eyes locked on ours, Kristen made little grunting noises that made us thankful for disposable diapers. "Uhhhh!" I wish I could accurately describe these noises with words, but I can't. I'm not sure anyone could.

Occasionally, Kristen would burst out into a loud, happy scream. She would throw her head back and laugh as loud as she could. She was genuinely excited about what we were doing and wanted to make us happy.

Our voices began to rise with anticipation as we encouraged her to take her first step. We were like a cheerleading squad at a basketball game, trying to help our team win the game. Our cheer went something like this:

"You can do it, Kristen, you can do it!" Clap! Clap!
"You can do it, Kristen, you can do it!" Clap! Clap!
"You can do it, Kristen, you can do it!" Clap! Clap!

Over and over we told her until her little body began to shake. Every part of her body above her ankles began to move with excitement. Each part shook and wiggled, but her feet never moved. It was as if her feet were glued to the floor. Her free hand would stretch out as far as it could toward us until her other hand could just barely touch the couch. Just when we thought she was going to let go of the couch and take her first step, she would fall to the floor in a sitting position, laughing as loud as she could.

What did we do? You guessed it. We stood her back up and encouraged her to try again. And try again she did.

Kristen tried and tried and eventually did walk, but not before she became an expert furniture walker. She would walk down each piece of furniture holding on with every step. When she came to the end of a couch or chair and couldn't walk any further, she would stop and survey the room looking for the next closest piece of furniture. Once she determined the piece of furniture closest to her in the direction she was going, she mustered her courage and darted as quickly as possible to it. She literally ran from one piece of furniture to the next until she got to where she wanted to go. With time and lots of encouragement, she finally let go of the furniture and moved from place to place without anyone's help. Just like Jonathan, Kristen overcame her fears and began to walk unassisted by having confidence in herself and believing she could do whatever she put her mind to.

With time and encouragement, all children become successful. As parents we convince them through our words and actions that they can do or be whatever they want to be. And one day something magical happens, and children begin to believe all the millions of supportive words they have heard spoken to them by their parents since their birth. They begin to believe in themselves. They are convinced they can do anything. They are full of confidence and no longer want our help. In fact, they demand that we leave them alone so they can do for themselves.

At this point, we begin to hear our words of encouragement repeated back to us. "I can do it!" "I can dress myself!" "I can pick out my own clothes!" "I can put my food on my plate!" "I can tie my own shoes!" "I don't need a baby-sitter!" "I can stay by myself!" "I can cross the street without your help!" "I don't need your help!" "I can do anything!" they say. For the first time our words—their words—scare us, and we see signs of our babies growing up and taking their first steps away from us.

After we spend years encouraging and convincing them that they can do and be anything they want to be, they have faith in themselves and begin to move away from us. They quit asking for our advice. They really don't care about our opinions anymore. They are confident in who they are and are convinced that they are in control of their own destinies.

They demonstrate this confidence in everything that they do. If they want to wear particular shirts and pants together, they put them on. They could care less whether we thought they went together or not. There have been many times when one of our children walked into our room two minutes before time to leave for school wearing clothes that obviously clashed with each other. As we looked at them, we never knew whether to laugh or cry. But that's what they wanted to wear, and there was no stopping them.

When eating meals, if they wanted more food on their plate, they got up from their chair and got it themselves. It didn't matter if they were not tall enough to see over the edge of the counter. It didn't matter that the stove might still be hot and they might burn themselves. It didn't matter that we offered to help them. They just took their spoons, reached up over their heads, and poked around until they found what they wanted. If we wanted to start an argument, just try helping them.

If they wanted to cross the street, they crossed it. It didn't matter one bit to them that we had told them a thousand times to never cross the street without us. They didn't care if the street was busy or not. They didn't care if we told them not to leave the yard. They had confidence in themselves, were convinced that they could do anything, and nothing, including their parents, could stop them.

As adults, few of us have this kind of confidence in ourselves anymore. Few believe we can do whatever we want to do or be whoever we want to be. Why is that? How can someone with so much confidence as a child have so little confidence as an adult?

From the time we begin to believe in ourselves, people—including our parents—begin to tear our confidence down. They tell us things like, "You can't do that!" "It's just not possible!" "Things just don't work that way!" "There's no way that you could understand what I mean!" "There are some things that you can't change!" "Things have always been done this way!" "Be happy with what you can do!" "Don't waste your time!" "You are making a big mistake!" "You don't have a chance!" Unfortunately, as adults, we often let other people convince us that we can no longer be successful, and we forget what it took and how successful we have been getting to this point in our lives. We erase from our memory and forget all the millions of success stories we wrote throughout our lifetimes that proved our worth and demonstrated our ability to do great things.

Just as we let our parents convince us that we can do anything, we begin to let others convince us that we can't. Just as we believe that nothing is bigger than we are, we begin to believe that everything is bigger than we can handle. Just as we know that we can be whoever we want to be, we are persuaded that we will never be more than we are. How can we let this happen?

There will always be people who will try to convince you that you are not capable of reaching your potential or following your dream. They will be looking for you at every turn and juncture of your life. They will give you all the best reasons why you can't do something. They will present you with every possible problem that you could ever encounter. They will follow you wherever you go and never give you rest.

They will use many disguises. They will disguise themselves as your friend, spouse, parent, sibling, partner, coworker, pastor, boss, neighbor, and anyone else convenient. And yes, they will come to you as a complete stranger, too. Recognize their disguises, and block them from your view. Never let one of these people distract or block you from accomplishing whatever you want to achieve.

Just as a horse wears blinders to keep him focused on where he is going, you must focus on your goals and not allow others to distract you from them. You must believe in yourself, block out all the distractions around you, and only focus on where you are going.

Children are good at blocking out all distractions. Have you ever tried to get the attention of a child who is watching her favorite television program? It was a waste of time trying to get Kristen's attention. You could set off an atomic bomb right beside her chair and she would never move. She purposely blocked out every distraction in the room and was totally focused on the television screen. Not until you stood in front of the television and completely blocked her view, would she even consider the possibility of focusing for even a second on something else. Even then, she still might try to look around you as if you weren't even there.

Learn to block out all distractions as you did when you were a child. Identify and eliminate all the people who try to distract you and tear you down. Stay focused on where you are going, and keep moving in that direction. Never let anything block your view of your destination or cause you to turn back.

If you want to be successful, you have to believe in yourself. You must have confidence in yourself just like when you were a child. You must believe without a doubt that you can do anything you put your mind to. When someone tells you that you can't do something, ask him or her why not? When someone tells you something is impossible, tell him or her nothing is impossible for you! When someone tells you that you are making a big mistake, tell him or her that you are not afraid to make mistakes if those mistakes take you where you want to go. When someone tells you that you are wasting your time, tell him or her that you don't waste your time, but use it to your best advantage. When someone tells you that this is the way it has always been done, and there is nothing you can do to change it, just say, "Watch me!"

Bottom-line, it's up to you. Success is within the reach of everyone. To get to this point in your life, you have already proven you can be successful. Nothing has changed since you were a child. As an adult, just as it was when you were a child, you can be anything you want to be. You can do anything you want to do. You only have to believe in yourself, and approach life with the same confidence you had as a child.

Success is for the taking for those who believe in themselves and are willing to reach out and take it.

Develop a Winning Attitude

Our attitude is the single most important factor determining our success. A good attitude will propel us towards our dream and will make our journey much more pleasant along the way. A poor attitude, on the other hand, will create detours and obstacles for us to overcome. Our attitude, a winning attitude, is the third fundamental element of being successful.

Success is always difficult for people with poor attitudes. They view every problem as a major catastrophe. When something doesn't go as planned, they stop functioning, lose sight of the objective, and quit trying. They are afraid to try anything new or different for fear it might not work. In the end, they would rather sit around and complain to everyone about why it didn't work and who's to blame.

You know people like this. They are the first to find problems with any new idea. They are the first to tell you why something won't work. They are the first to complain when something goes wrong. They are the first to tell you "I told you so" when everything doesn't go as planned.

However, there are several things these people will almost never do. They are rarely the first to suggest a new idea to make something better. If they suggest an idea, be assured it will only benefit them and no one else. They are seldom interested in making a process better but in making their involvement in the process easier.

Second, they rarely say, "That's a great idea," before the idea is developed and proven. An idea that doesn't come from them is hardly ever a good idea. If an idea other than theirs is used, you can bet your last dollar they will not buy into the idea. They will wait until the idea has gotten rave reviews from everyone and has been deemed a success before they will lend their support.

Third, they will hardly ever be the first to try something different when something doesn't work as it should. In fact, they will continue to do it incorrectly just because they told you before you started that it wouldn't work. When confronted about their actions and about why they didn't try something else, they will give a lame excuse about how they were only doing what they were told to do.

Finally, they rarely take the blame for anything that goes wrong. Nothing is ever their fault. They seldom take responsibility for their own actions but blame others when things don't go their way.

A poor attitude will not only affect your own degree of success, but will also affect the success of those around you. The main goal of people with poor attitudes is to make you as miserable as they are. They are prepared to do whatever is necessary to accomplish this. They will exaggerate the truth, spread rumors, and whine about everything. It somehow makes them feel better when someone else shares in their misery. The Osmond Brothers coined it correctly in their hit song "One Bad Apple." Just as the song relates to relationships and love, the same is true of a bad attitude; one person with a poor attitude can spoil the success of the entire group.

Contrary to a poor attitude, a good attitude is the single most important factor influencing your ability to fulfill your dreams and be successful. It is more important than knowledge, experience, or financial resources. However, I'm not talking about a positive attitude; I am describing a winning attitude.

A positive attitude works under the premise that whatever happens you are to grin and bear it. Nothing will keep you from being happy. A smile stays glued to your face at all times. You speak in a calm and uplifting voice. You whistle when you walk and can't understand why others don't join in.

You've seen people who claim to have a positive attitude. They are always telling you what a great day it is. Some listen to subliminal tapes to purge themselves of all their negative thoughts. When you ask them how they are doing, they tell you, "Terrific!" "I have never been better!" they say. They lead you to believe that positive vibes run throughout their bodies. That is until they run into a problem they can't grin and bear, even with all of their positive indoctrinations. Then it all breaks loose. The floodwalls come crashing down, and they pitch hissy fits just like the rest of us do when something goes wrong. Their radiant smiles turn to ugly frowns. Their never-before-wrinkled foreheads scrunch up. Negative words spew from their mouths. And when you ask them if they are all right, they tell you to butt out and leave them alone. A once perfect day is ruined.

Let's be realistic, it is impossible to maintain a positive attitude all the time. No matter how hard you try, there will always be times when something goes wrong, attempting to ruin your day. For example, it's a cold winter day and you're running late for work. As you get out of your car, you close the door on your coat. As you reach for the door handle, you notice out of the corner of you eye your car keys dangling from the ignition switch. You pull on the door handle hoping it didn't lock, but it did. You pull and pull on your coat, but it won't come free. As a last resort, you strip off your coat and leave it hanging in the door. As you run toward your building, you slip on the ice and fall. Of course, your first reaction, regardless of your injuries, is to get up as quickly as possible while checking to see if anyone saw you fall. Once you determine no one is watching, you breathe a sigh of relief and realize that your pants are torn, and your knee is bleeding. You grumble under your breath as you limp into work fifteen minutes late.

Now, no one would expect you to have a positive attitude after what just happened. I'm afraid telling coworkers that you were having a wonderful day at this point would only draw strange stares. They wouldn't expect you to be all cheery and happy about life and probably wouldn't believe you if you were.

No matter what we do or how we condition ourselves to think positively, we are going to have things happen to us every day that won't make us feel very positive. We get stuck in traffic and miss an important appointment. We miss an urgent call from a potential client. Our favorite team loses the championship game. We break an antique crystal glass that has been handed down in our family for generations. Our purse or wallet is stolen while eating lunch with old friends. None of these things make us feel positive but only add to our frustration.

Maintaining a positive attitude all the time is not possible. Not only is it not possible, it is not the answer to being successful. Only a winning attitude will get us through the challenges we face each day and allow us to be successful at everything we do.

So what's a winning attitude? A winning attitude is an attitude that acknowledges the fact that there are going to always be things that happen that will cause us to stumble and fall. It also realizes that during these times, we are not going to be very positive. But a winning attitude differs from a positive attitude in that, no matter what happens or how bad things get, we acknowledge our frustration, pick ourselves up, brush ourselves off, and try again. That's a winning attitude.

Having a winning attitude takes practice. It doesn't come easy. There are going to be days when Murphy's Law will be waiting around every corner to knock you down. When it does, you're allowed to be negative for one minute. During this minute, you can have the biggest pity party ever held. You can feel sorry for yourself, cry, scream, pout, take a walk, throw things—not at someone I hope—or do anything else that relieves your frustration and makes you feel better. For sixty seconds you can do anything you want to express you anger and disappointment. But at the end of that minute, you have to pick yourself up, brush yourself off, and try again.

We built a fence around our backyard when Jonathan was two. Because we lived on a heavily traveled road, we were afraid he would slip away from us one day while our backs were turned and go into the street. We felt the fence was best for his protection and our peace of mind.

For several days after the fence was installed he walked the perimeter of the four-foot, chain-link fence looking for a way out. Like all children, Jonathan loved to play outside and explore his space and didn't want to be restricted in any way. Every so often, as he walked down the fence line, he would stop and grab the fence, shake it as hard as he could, and mumble something to himself. After about a minute, he would continue walking down the fence.

For ease of access to the yard, we had three gates installed. They had the regular gate latches that all chain link fences have to secure the gate.

Jonathan wasn't very tall at the time, and we didn't feel it was necessary to lock them. Of course, that feeling changed very quickly.

One day my wife left Jonathan playing in the backyard while she went to answer the phone. When she returned less than a minute later, the gate was open, and Jonathan was gone. How did he get the gate open? Did we forget to latch the gate? Did one of the neighborhood kids open the gate and let him out? Luckily, my wife found him in the next-door neighbor's yard chasing a cat.

From that day forward, we watched Jonathan very carefully while he played in the yard. Still unsure of how the gate opened, we were afraid to leave him alone for any length of time.

One day while my wife watched him out our kitchen window, Jonathan gave himself away. He grabbed a stick laying in the yard, and in prison-break fashion, pushed up the handle, opened the gate, and scurried out of the yard.

From that point forward, the gate was always locked. At first we used a ten-penny nail bent into the shape of an upside down "v" placed in the latch. Within ten minutes after we put the bent nail in the gate, Jonathan began to push up on the handle with a stick. But this time it didn't open.

Jonathan was furious. He grunted loudly, screamed, and threw himself to the ground in anger. In about a minute, he got up, found his stick, and tried pushing up on the handle again. When this didn't work, he threw himself to the ground again, kicking and screaming. Nothing seemed to work for Jonathan.

A few days later while my wife and I worked in the yard, we heard the gate open. Jonathan had taken one of his toys and knocked the nail out of the latch, and in one swift motion, pushed up the handle. As he ran out of the yard, he looked over his shoulder at us with a smile that stretched from ear to ear.

For the next few weeks, we tried several different things in the latch to keep Jonathan from opening the gate. We tried bending the nail in different shapes, parachute clips, and rope tied in every possible knot. Nothing seemed to work. For every new thing we tried, Jonathan tried something else and was able to open the gate.

Over time, it became a family challenge. For my wife and me, it became a challenge to keep Jonathan in the fence and still allow access in and out of the yard. For Jonathan, it became a challenge to break our new locking system and escape his boundaries.

Each time Jonathan tried what had worked the time before. If Jonathan's old method of opening the gate didn't work any longer, he threw himself to the ground in a fit of rage. A short time later—about a minute—he stopped his rage, got up, and tried something else. This family challenge went on all summer.

As a last resort, to keep Jonathan inside the fence, we locked the gates with pad locks. You know the one they shoot on television with a high-powered rifle and it stays locked. Jonathan quickly learned the lock didn't open when he hit it with a stick, either.

I would like to tell you this was the end of the story, but it's not. A few days later, my wife caught Jonathan half way over the fence, climbing to freedom. When the gate no longer opened, Jonathan found a new way to get out of the fence; he climbed over.

You see, as challenging as it was that summer to keep Jonathan in the confines of our backyard, for whatever reason, he was never content with being limited to the area inside the fence. Jonathan wanted to play outside the fence and was determined not the let the fence prevent him from doing so. In his own way, he made it his goal that summer to find a way out of the fence, despite whatever my wife and I concocted to confine him to the safety of our backyard. Because of his determination, you might say that Jonathan had a winning attitude. He could have easily given up after each time he failed to open the gate, but he didn't. He could have told himself getting outside the fence was hopeless, and there wasn't any use in trying. He could have had a continuous pity party and made everyone around him miserable. He could have blamed everybody but himself for his failures, but he didn't. He never let anything my wife and I tried that summer stop him from attempting to get out of our backyard.

Children are that way. Every time they have something they want to do or accomplish, they don't let every little obstacle stop them. They don't let rules, locked gates, or even well-meaning parents get in their way. They do whatever it takes to reach their objectives.

They get mad—for about a minute—and throw a big temper fit. They cry. They scream. They throw themselves to the ground. When it is all said and done, they get up as if it never happened and try again.

In Jonathan's case, he made it his personal objective to get outside the fence. For days he walked the fence perimeter looking for a way out. Once he discovered the gate, he used a stick to open the latch. He didn't let the nail or any of the other things my wife and I tried stop him. Once we installed the locks, and he couldn't open the gates, he began to climb the fence. Throughout this process, he had many setbacks, disappointments, and failures. He would spend hours at a time trying different things. And yes, he threw temper tantrums when things didn't go as he thought they should but never for very long. After each failure he picked himself up, brushed himself off, and tried again.

That's what people with winning attitudes do. When things don't go the way they think they should, they don't quit and give up; they try something different. They don't look for others to blame when things go wrong. They take responsibility for their actions and try to make things right. They pick themselves up, brush themselves off, and try again.

As an elementary student, Jonathan played full-contact football in the local city league. Because of his size and speed, he played a running back position, a position he dearly loved.

As anyone with football experience knows, being a running back is not easy. Eleven players on the other side of the ball focus all their attention on you. They hit, push, grab, and do whatever is necessary to keep you from scoring.

As nature would have it, each year the boys get a little bigger. At thirteen, Jonathan went up against boys twice his height and weight. You would think that playing against players twice his size would be a problem for him, but it wasn't. To Jonathan's detriment, he was not afraid of anyone.

Jonathan took some hard hits over the years. Many times after a hard tackle, my wife and I were certain Jonathan would never get up, but he always did. He got up, brushed himself off, and ran back to the huddle to get his next assignment.

From the time the whistle blows to stop the previous play until the next play starts, fits of rage occur all over the field. For about a minute, players butt heads, slap high fives, and scream at the top of their lungs. Butts are whacked, shoulder pads are hit, and the coach's voice can be heard across the field, shouting instructions to his players. As quick as the play starts, it ends.

In less than a minute, the players come out of the huddle with their new assignments ready for the next play. As they position themselves at the line of scrimmage, each player is ready to do battle again, with only distant memories of the previous play. They don't dwell on their mistakes from the last play. They pick themselves up, brush themselves off, devise a new plan of attack, and try again. So must you!

To be successful at anything, you must have a winning attitude. An attitude that is not afraid to fail, but accepts failure as part of life. An attitude that is not afraid to get mad or be negative when things are not going well but, within a minute, is willing to forget the disappointment, devise a new plan or approach and try again.

People with winning attitudes don't look for others to blame. People with winning attitudes blame themselves for their failures and treat each failure as a learning experience.

People with winning attitudes don't quit at the first signs of trouble or give up when life knocks them down. They pick themselves up, brush themselves off, and try again.

As UCLA Bruins' former football Coach Henry Russell ("Red") Sanders once said, "Winning isn't everything. It's the only thing!" To be successful at everything you do, you must have a winning attitude like you had as a child. You must never give up when you face failure or disappointment; you must keep moving forward toward your goal. As such, a winning attitude is the third fundamental element of the building blocks of success.

Be Adaptable

To be successful at anything, you must be adaptable. You must be willing to change with the wind and adapt to whatever life throws at you. This is the fourth fundamental element of the building blocks of success.

A baby knows this better than anyone does. At the moment of birth, a baby instantly converts from breathing seminal fluid to breathing air. It goes from a warm and dark environment to a cold and bright room. Its method of feeding changes from an intravenous tube attached to its stomach to a mother's breast. Does the baby complain? Maybe a little, but it knows by instinct that to survive, it must adapt to its new environment quickly.

In the first few weeks, the baby begins to regulate its bodily functions. Its breathing, heartbeat, and temperature begin to stabilize. Its sleeping pattern begins to adjust and it is awake for longer periods of time. Its eyes begin to open wide and focus on your face. Little noises other than those used for crying begin to emerge.

After only a few months, the baby is no longer stationary, but becomes mobile as it learns to crawl. When this happens, sitting in one spot is no longer good enough. It raises itself up on its hands and knees, rocking back and forth as if that would propel him or her forward. It doesn't. It only causes the baby to occasionally fall flat on its face, screaming in disapproval.

Within a short period of time, the baby learns from its mistakes. It coordinates its arms with its legs and moves around on all fours, seeking out things that could only be stared at from across the room a short time ago.

It's not long before the baby quickly realizes that the better things in life are stored on a table or shelf, not on the floor. As a result, the baby learns to pull itself up and stand on its own two feet, reaching as far as it can reach with one hand as the other hand holds on for dear life to a stationary object. Seeing everything it can see. Grabbing everything it can grab.

Within a year the baby shows signs of walking and distinct communication skills. The baby begins to walk beside the furniture to get where it is going—holding on every step of the way. Two-way communications between the adult and child begin to form, as the baby no longer has to point and grunt but is able to form simple words to get across his or her meaning.

By the time the baby is two years old, it is defiant and into everything. Nothing is off limits. Everything is for the taking. The baby refuses to accept no from anyone.

I remember Jonathan when he was two. He was into everything. Nothing could keep him from where he wanted to be. Telling Jonathan no was a waste of time. If he wanted it, as soon as we turned our back, it was his.

Once Jonathan was able to move from one place to another, we bought door locks for all our kitchen cabinets. You know those simple but effective contraptions you install on the inside of the cabinet doors to keep your child from getting into something that they shouldn't get into. They work really well, especially on adults.

My wife and I had the hardest time opening our cabinets after we installed the locks. It was like breaking into Fort Knox every time we had to open a door. We got to the point where we hated to open a door and avoided it whenever possible. However, we believed the locks would surely keep Jonathan out of the cabinets, too. We know now that we should never say surely when it comes to a child.

In quick order, Jonathan began to pull at the locked doors. He was like a wild man in a cage trying to break out. We could hear the door locks rattle all over the house as Jonathan jerked the doors back and forth against the locks. The mere fact that the locks were keeping Jonathan from opening the doors seemed to make him work harder trying to open them. The pots and pans he so fondly liked to play with were no longer at his disposal—locked behind closed doors out of reach. My wife and I smiled with content, knowing we had protected our child from the dangers lurking behind each door.

However, our smiles were short lived. Like I said before, nothing is off limits to a determined two-year-old child, and Jonathan was no different. It wasn't but a few days later when Jonathan figured out the locking mechanisms and began to open the doors. Jonathan no longer stood wildly pulling at the doors. There were no longer any banging noises. There was only a little hand slipping through the cracks of the doors to unlatch the locks. My two-year-old son was doing something with great ease that was difficult for my wife and me to do.

By three, a baby is able to make choices. He or she is able to pick between likes and dislikes. It is able to choose what it wants to wear as well as what it wants to eat. The baby is prepared to make choices for itself. It not only requests but also demands that its parents allow it to do so.

Around the age of five or six, a child starts school and begins a formal, structured, learning process. The child learns to read, write, and do simple math. It learns to stand in a line and to form a circle. The child learns to play games with other children and differentiate between winning and losing. It begins to develop friendships that may last a lifetime.

At thirteen, the child becomes a teenager and starts to leave childhood behind. In the next few years, its body goes through tremendous change—both physical and mental—as it reaches puberty. Its childlike body starts to transform into the adult body that will carry it through the rest of its life.

Before you know it, the child is an adult just like you and me. In just a few short years, it develops from a small bundle of flesh struggling for its very existence to a teenager beginning the first steps of adulthood—growing and adapting as fast as before. Changing like the wind it adapts and adjusts to whatever life throws at it.

It seems like yesterday when Jonathan was born. Jonathan was our first child, and we wanted to do all the right things. Everything the doctor told us, we followed to a tee. We took everything he said literally as we sat on the edge of our chairs listening to every word and instruction.

We read books to learn everything we could about this little bundle of joy that would soon arrive. Because our families were two states away and too far from us to help in an emergency, we only had a short period of time to become experts on this little baby before it was born. So we read. And we read. And we read.

Toward the last part of my wife's pregnancy, we enrolled in a Lamaze class. We had discussed throughout her pregnancy the benefits of going natural, and we decided to try. It was an easy decision for me. However, it was one decision that I would later regret.

The class was so much fun, and we looked forward to going each week. Practicing the breathing techniques and exercises always provided a good laugh. It was quite a sight seeing thirty very pregnant women lying on the floor like beached whales with their heads resting against their husbands' chests. Each woman was gasping for breath like a dying person in a movie while practicing breathing patterns. The best laugh was watching each one get up off the floor when we were through.

When we weren't practicing our breathing patterns, we were watching films. I'll be honest. I wasn't ready for some of the films. They were more intense than I had imagined and at times made me reconsider our decision to go natural. But my wife was convinced it was the right thing to do, and since I was not the one who would actually be feeling the pain—or so I thought—I agreed.

During our last class, we visited the local hospital for a tour of where we would go when the time arrived. The instructors went over all the hospital procedures and the rules the husbands were to follow. We went over simple things like where to park, which door to enter, where the father could not go, where to admit the mother, and so forth. They showed us the labor room where my wife would relax until time for the birth. They showed us the birthing room where the actual birth would take place. It was an informative discussion, describing the organization and simplicity of the process. Of course, as you may have already guessed, it didn't work that way for us.

My wife had a fairly easy pregnancy. She had been sick very little and didn't experience much discomfort until the last few weeks. She practiced her Lamaze exercises religiously each day and was ready for whatever was to happen.

Our doctor monitored her pregnancy weekly and told us everything was going well. After all—he told us—this was our first child, and we had plenty of time to get to the hospital. He persuaded us that once the labor pains started, we shouldn't even consider coming to the hospital until the labor pains were five minutes apart for an hour. It would be many hours before the baby would be born and we shouldn't be in any hurry.

Now, my wife and I were not so confident and worried about the time between labor pains much more than our doctor did. The hospital was in Bowling Green, Kentucky, and we lived in Franklin, a small town about twenty miles south of Bowling Green. Throughout the pregnancy we made many timed trips from our house to the hospital and could make it there in about twenty-three minutes. That is, if everything went as planned.

The day that we had anticipated for months finally arrived. My wife started having labor pains early that morning, and because the doctor said we had plenty of time, I went on to work. I left with the understanding that when her labor pains got to thirty minutes apart she would call me, and I would come home.

It wasn't long before my wife called. She said she was doing okay. Her pains were thirty minutes apart, and she told me to take my time coming home because we had plenty of time. I was so excited that our first child was about to be born; I ignored my wife and hurried home. I'm glad I did.

By the time I got there—about ten minutes later—her labor pains were five minutes apart. She had two more at five minutes apart, and then they jumped to two minutes. This was not the way it was supposed to happen! The doctor had said we would have plenty of time! We decided to call him. He acted as surprised as we were but didn't display any tone of urgency in his voice. He told us, again, that we had plenty of time, but to play it safe he told us to meet him at the hospital. And that's just what we did.

We grabbed my wife's packed go-bag with all of her clothes and our Lamaze supplies and headed for the hospital. With the four-way flashers flashing and the speedometer needle over as far as it would go, we made the twenty-three minute trip to the hospital in twelve minutes—a record that still stands today. We ran red lights, ran stop signs, and passed people on the wrong side of the road. It wasn't until we got to downtown Bowling Green that we ran into problems.

About a mile from the hospital, we were stuck in traffic at a red light. The next three minutes were the longest three minutes of my life. While sitting at the red light, my wife had a major labor pain. She began to bang on the passenger door with her fist as hard as she could. A wet rag hung from her mouth—a Lamaze technique to keep the mouth moist with water—as she screamed at the top of her lungs. An elderly lady sitting beside us in a truck stared intently at us and began to roll down her window to get a closer look. You could see in her face what she was thinking. Was I holding this woman against her will? Was the man in the car attacking her? What was going on over there? Just as she was about to say something, the light turned green, and we quickly sped away.

Within another two minutes, we were screeching up in the driveway of the hospital. I didn't even look to see if there was a parking space available in the lot we were supposed to park in. My only thoughts were to get as close to the door as possible.

As quickly as I could, I got my wife out of the car and headed for the door. The door was the entrance to a waiting area where children had to wait while their parents visited someone in the hospital. There were children everywhere playing and having a good time.

The real fun began when my wife entered the waiting room. About midway across the room, as we headed toward the elevator, she had another labor pain and hollered at the top of her lungs. The children stopped playing instantly and scattered in every direction. It was if the children were playing hide-and-seek with my wife and she just finished counting to ten. They ran for their lives, avoiding my wife at all costs. With one scream, my wife turned a room filled with happy children into a room filled with frightened children, hiding behind chairs, plants, and couches.

Thank goodness that the nurses weren't running away. A wonderful nurse from the maternity ward was getting off work, saw what was happening, and asked if she could help us. The nice lady—I wish I knew her name—comforted my wife and told us that everything was going to be all right. She told me to go ahead and park the car, admit my wife into the hospital, and she would help my wife get to where she needed to be. She assured us that we had plenty of time.

A few minutes later while I stood in line to admit my wife, the telephone rang. From behind a wall, I could hear a voice calling my name. "Is there a Mr. Muse in here?" she asked. I quickly moved to the front of the line and a staff member told me to go straight to delivery. My wife was ready to deliver and refused to have the baby until I arrived.

I ran to the elevator and went up to the Maternity Ward where a nurse was waiting for me. "Are you Mr. Muse?" she asked in an excited voice. I said yes, and she quickly took me behind the closed doors I wasn't supposed to go behind.

The next few seconds were what I could only imagine a firefighter goes through when the firehouse alarm sounds. After scrubbing my hands, we literally ran down a long hallway past all the other labor rooms where my wife was originally scheduled to rest until delivery while I put on the medical garb—the hat, the pants, the gown, and the shoe coverings, never stopping our run down the hallway. As we opened the door to where my wife was laying, the nurse tied the final knot on my mask behind my head.

Within seconds, my son was born. He lay on my wife's stomach as she dosed in and out of a restful sleep. We had our first child, and my wife did it as natural as possible. It happened so quickly that the doctors didn't have time to administer any drugs to ease the pain. So much for plenty of time!

As soon as it was over, my wife's pain seemed to go away. On the other hand, my pain was only beginning. During her final push, she grabbed the collar of my shirt and pulled my face close to hers. In the process, she choked me pretty good and left my neck stiff. I will never forget the look in her eyes. I only saw that look one other time in thirty-three years of marriage—two years later when my daughter was born.

However, Kristen's birth was much different. Unlike Jonathan, she was more laid-back about coming into this world. Because of our experience with Jonathan's birth, our doctor told us to leave for the hospital as soon as my wife started having labor pains. But this time around, Kristen was in no hurry. We spent most of the day in the labor room waiting for Kristen to arrive. Although different, we were just as excited about her birth and thanked God for her.

I can't fully explain how I felt at those moments when my children were born. With Jonathan, my wife had just given birth to a healthy baby boy. I cried with joy and, at the same time, feared the responsibility that a child would bring to my life. I wondered if I was ready to be a father and make the decisions that a father must make. I worried how the arrival of our child would change my relationship with my wife. Change is a scary thing even to those who think they are ready for it.

Within minutes, Jonathan began to adapt to his new life and environment. The change in his life seemed to have no effect on him at all. He settled in and became comfortable in his new surroundings. He quit crying, he urinated all over a nurse—that's a good thing they told us—and he fell fast asleep before the rest of us could even catch our breath.

Over the next several years, Jonathan adapted well to his new life and went through five distinct stages or changes of development. There were other stages, but these stages were the most meaningful to my wife and me. He instinctively took each change in stride, adding each one to his experiences as he prepared himself for whatever life had in store for him next.

The first major change I remember was when Jonathan began to feed himself. This was a joyous occasion for my wife and me. We no longer had to eat in shifts, and we could all sit down together to eat as a family. This had not happened since he had been born, and it helped us regain some freedom we had lost. Best of all, my wife and I could once again feel comfortable going out to restaurants.

Jonathan loved the change. He was messy at first and missed his mouth from time to time, but he was feeding himself. He was never quite sure where his mouth was in relation to his spoon, but he was happy. He was having the best time of his life. The fact that the food was all over him bothered my wife and me much more than it ever bothered Jonathan.

The next major change occurred when Jonathan began to talk. From the day he was born, Jonathan used different cries to mean different things. There was a cry when he was tired. There was a different cry for when he was hurt. There was a cry he used when he was hungry. When he began to talk, things got much easier. We no longer had to guess or try to interpret why he was crying. He could tell us. He could tell us when he was sleepy and wanted to go to bed. He could tell us where he was hurting, and we could comfort him much sooner. He could tell us that he was hungry and what he wanted to eat.

The third major change came when Jonathan started walking. We no longer had to carry him when we wanted to go somewhere. We didn't have to carry his stroller wherever we went. He could walk on his own, and he was happy to do it. My wife and I were happy as well.

Another stage of change occurred when Jonathan no longer needed diapers. For those of you who are not parents yet, diapers are expensive. They are the most expensive item a baby uses and are more expensive than food or clothing. On an average day, Jonathan could go through ten of them without even working up a sweat.

The expense was only part of the problem. They are messy. You haven't lived until you have changed a runny diaper that has spilled out the leg holes or smelled a diaper pail that has a few days of diapers stuffed in it. The flushing sound of the toilet was music to our ears when Jonathan started using it. In addition, we were able to get rid of the diaper bag that had almost become permanently attached to our shoulders.

The fifth stage of change started when Jonathan began to dress himself. Do you know how much time this saved my wife and me? Do you realize how much later we were able to sleep each morning when we didn't have to get up and dress Jonathan? It made him feel so big when he dressed himself, and we were willing to let him feel as big as he wanted.

Of course, we were as happy as Jonathan was about his development, but undesirable things came along with each stage of change. When Jonathan started feeding himself, it seemed like we were constantly changing his clothes. He was so messy after every meal and had to be changed almost every time he left the table.

When he learned to talk, he never stopped. He talked all the time. From the time he got up in the morning until he went to bed at night, he was constantly talking.

When Jonathan started walking, we could never keep up with him. If we turned our backs for a split second, he was gone. I don't know how many times we thought we had lost him while we were shopping.

When he quit needing diapers, we had to start letting him use the bathroom wherever we went. It didn't matter where we were or how long it had been since he had used the bathroom last, he had to go. He had to use every bathroom he saw.

When Jonathan started dressing himself, he took his ever-loving time when we had to go somewhere he didn't want to go. He would play a while. He would dress a while. It was his way of letting us know he was not happy with our travel plans.

That's the way change is. It can be good as well as bad at the same time. How we react and adapt to change is what makes the difference. Those who look at change as a problem are constantly disappointed about the way things are going. Conversely, those who look at change as an opportunity and are willing to adapt and adjust, rule the world. Those people rarely look back to see where they have been but look forward toward where they are going.

If you want to be successful, you have to adapt as you did when you were a child. You have to be willing to change direction at the drop of a hat. You have to adapt to whatever situation you face. Let's face it; things that make you successful today may not make you successful tomorrow.

Success is a moving target. It doesn't sit still and wait for you. Likewise, you can't sit still and wait for it. It is constantly moving in first one direction and then the other. To catch success, you must be willing to move with it.

Now, I'm not a hunter, but from shooting at moving targets at the state fair, I have learned a little about the process. To be able to hit the target you have to move with it. If your target moves to the left, you have to move your gun to the left. You have to keep your eye on the moving target at all times to keep it in your gun sights. If it moves to the right, you have to move to the right. If it speeds up or slows down, you have to do the same. Whichever way the target moves, you have to adapt and move with it.

After you have played the game a while, you begin to think that you can anticipate the target's next move. You fix your sights on a place ahead of the target waiting for the target to pass by. I can tell you from experience that this method doesn't always work. Just as the target is about to cross in front of your sight, it veers off into another direction and leaves you standing there with nothing to shoot at. It acts as if it knew you were there waiting. On the rare occasion that it does pass by, it passes by so quickly that you don't have time to aim and shoot. At best, you shoot and miss.

To succeed at hitting the target and reaching your goal, you have to adapt and adjust to its every move. When it moves, you have to move with it. When it stops, you have to stop. Whatever it does or whatever change it makes, you have to adapt and change with it.

Babies are masters of change and adaptability. Within a few short years, they develop and adapt to meet every challenge of life. They learn to walk and talk. They learn to feed themselves and change their own clothes. They learn to control their bodily functions as they adapt to the world around them.

You must also adapt. Your success depends on it. The next time life throws a curve ball at you, look at it as you did when you were a child, and create an opportunity, not a problem. Life is too short to create problems. You must be willing to change with the wind, adjust, and take advantage of every opportunity that life might throw at you. Life is full of opportunities for those who are willing to adapt and change to meet them.

Never Stop Learning

The next basic element of success relates to how we approach life and how important the collection of information and knowledge is. Constantly learning new things lays the groundwork for future successes and shortens the path to your final destination. Therefore, learning everything you can is the fifth fundamental element of the building blocks of success.

Go back with me a second. Do you remember how you learned about new things when you were a child? Can you remember how excited you were when someone or something turned the light bulb on in your head? Can you remember how you used that knowledge, that information to be successful as a child? For example, can you remember the first time you tied your shoes or rode your bike without anyone's help? Can you remember the first time you crossed the street by yourself? Can you remember when you learned to read your first book? Learning was fun! You couldn't wait to learn about something new. Are you just excited about learning new things as an adult? If you're not, you should be. Learning new things is fundamental to being successful and being able to do whatever you want to do.

The phrase "knowledge is power" is correct—as trite as this saying may sound. The more knowledge you have about anything the more power and insight you have to help you make better decisions in all phases of your life.

The learning process is the same today as an adult as it was when you were a child. How did you learn new things as a child? Children learn about the world they live in four different ways: they break things, they learn from their mistakes, they learn from other successful children, and if they don't know something, they ask questions. These four basic methods children use to learn new things are the same methods you use to learn things you need to know as an adult. Learning everything you can is not only a fundamental element of the building blocks of success, it gives you the power and knowledge you need to be successful at everything you do. Let's look at each one in more detail.

Children Break Things

From the moment my son was born, he had a curiosity for tools and for how things worked. You've heard about kids who were born with a silver spoon in their mouth Well, my son was born with a screwdriver in his hand. As soon as he began to talk, he started asking questions. "How does this work?" What does this do?" "Why does this work this way?" His curiosity and thirst for knowledge were unquenchable.

Of course, his curiosity about how things worked created quite a challenge for my wife and me. Fielding questions about the inner-workings of particular items all day—every day—after a while, made us feel inadequate. As he got older, his questions became more and more difficult, and he was never satisfied with a standard, pat answer. He would never let us get away with responses such as "that's just the way it works" or "this part works with that part." Generalizations would never do. He wanted details. He wanted to know the name of every part and about how each part worked with every other part.

Thankfully, we got a lot of help from my wife's family, especially her father. Several men in her family with engineering backgrounds were willing to sit for hours at a time answering Jonathan's questions. They were all amazed at his inquisitiveness and had just as much fun explaining how things worked as Jonathan had listening to their explanations.

I will never forget the time when Jonathan was about four years old. My wife's father, affectionately known as Paw Paw to my children, spent an entire evening explaining to him how an internal combustion engine works. Just to say that it had pistons that went up and down was not good enough. Jonathan wanted to know about every part, where every part was located, and what every part did. He made my father-in-law draw diagrams of how the parts moved in relationship to the other parts. Jonathan made Paw Paw take him outside and open the hood of his car to show him the parts on an actual working engine. Once he understood one part of the engine, they moved on to something else.

I know what you're thinking. How can a four-year-old understand the inner workings of an internal combustion engine? To be honest, I don't know. Our family asked the same question many times. To this day, I still do not fully understand how an engine works. I know that pistons go up and down, where small controlled explosions occur, and a few other things, but that's about it. So how did Jonathan understand such a complex machine? It was simple. He wanted to know how it worked more than anything else. If you told him something he didn't understand, he would keep asking questions until you phrased your answer in such a way that he could. His desire for knowledge transcended his ability to understand. Do I think he totally understood everything he was told? No, but he understood to the best of his ability and was never satisfied until he reached that point.

Jonathan especially enjoyed repair people. When they came to our home to fix things, he would stay right underfoot watching every move asking questions about every step. He became their personal helper and would hand tools to them when requested.

Surprisingly, most of the repair people accepted Jonathan and didn't mind him tagging along. They answered all of his questions and treated him as a coworker. Some treated him like a son.

It wasn't long before our answers were no longer good enough. My family just couldn't give the details he wanted. About this same time, we bought Jonathan a small tool set. Because of his natural curiosity to understand how things worked, we felt it was a natural progression for him to have his own tools. He had always been interested in my tools and left them all over the house when he pretended to work on things. Who knows, I reasoned, by giving him his own tools, he might just leave mine alone. In retrospect, this was a purchase that I learned to regret from time to time as he got older.

Jonathan has always been good with his hands. His dexterity and eye-hand coordination developed very quickly and seemed to be ahead of children his same age. Even at an early age, he was good at building things with blocks and putting shaped objects through the corresponding holes. In fact, he wasn't just good; he was very good.

His first tool set was a basic set of tools: a few screwdrivers, a set of pliers, and a crescent wrench. We didn't get a hammer on purpose. My wife and I were afraid he might decide to use it on someone one day. He didn't seem to notice he didn't have a hammer and didn't seem to mind.

As a result of this purchase, an instant love relationship developed. Jonathan loved his tools. Everywhere Jonathan went his tool set went too. They were inseparable. He was so cute going around with his little toolbox asking everyone if there was anything he could fix. Little did we know at the time that he had no intentions of fixing anything.

In short order he began to take everything apart. He began to dismantle every toy he owned, both old and new. Once he established what the toy could do and had a basic understanding of how it worked, it was scheduled for dismantle. Nothing was off limits. He reduced everything to its most basic elements, not allowing any two parts to remain together. He would examine each part with care and set it to the side.

At first my wife and I were extremely concerned about his activities. We tried to put several of the toys back together as best we could, but it was no use. In the time we could have a toy back together he could have two apart. We struggled to determine what parts went with what toys. The simplest of toys became complicated when we didn't know if we even had all the right parts. No matter how hard we worked to stay ahead of him, it became quickly apparent to us that he didn't want his toys intact. As soon as we reassembled one, he would take it apart.

Talking to him about the situation was a waste of time. He was so intent on knowing how each toy worked that he was willing to sacrifice each, one by one. Within a few months, that's just about what he did. Instead of shelves of nice toys, he had boxes of toy parts. Instead of toys that worked, he had toys that he worked on. Instead of having original toys that might be collectibles someday, he had toys made from parts of other toys. Instead of having the latest and hottest toys that any child would be proud of, he had remnants of toys he had made the day before. Was he happy with the situation that he had created for himself? He was happy as a lark.

I wish I could tell you that it stopped with his toys, but it didn't. One day at lunch while I was talking with my daughter at the kitchen table—our normal workday routine—I heard Jonathan's tools banging together in the next room. For some reason Kristen was especially talkative that day, and the noise of Jonathan's tools didn't grab my attention—at least not at first.

As I walked into the next room to kiss Jonathan goodbye before I went back to work, I just about passed out. Spread all over the floor of the living room was my twenty-five-inch console color television still plugged in—aaahhhh! Jonathan had placed each part in neat rows around the cabinet. He sat in the middle of the parts with his screwdriver in his left hand.

Needless to say, I went ballistic. I ranted and raved, and yes, I spanked him, which didn't make either one of us feel any better. I was so mad that I told him he had better have the television back together before I got home—not really meaning it—or he would get spanked again.

On the way back to work I tried to calm down, but the thought of Jonathan taking the television apart while I sat in the next room talking to Kristen controlled my thoughts. Why must he take everything apart? Why is it so important to him that he knows how everything works? He could have died!

Even as a teenager, Jonathan took everything apart. His thirst for knowledge of how things work has never ceased. He had a workbench in our basement stacked with various parts of different things. Projects of intermixed parts were piled high on several shelves. He cluttered his workbench with items in different stages of disassembly and repair.

I admit Jonathan's desire to tear everything apart and to know how things work is much stronger than most. But most children, no matter how they express it, exhibit the same thirst for knowledge. If something is important to them and interests them, they cannot and will not be happy until they know everything about it. If it means tearing something apart to see how it works, they will do it without even thinking about it. It doesn't matter to children how much the toys cost or their possible future value. It doesn't matter that you spent every lunch hour for a week going to stores all over town to find that particular toy. It doesn't matter about the long lines you had to stand in to purchase it. To Jonathan the toy was insignificant. Only the knowledge he could gain from it was important.

Why do we lose the desire for knowledge as we get older? Why do we, at some point in life, become content with our knowledge level and are not willing to learn anything new? Why are we at times happy with what we know and are willing to die by our old ways? Only you can answer these questions for yourself. Everyone has different reasons to quit learning, but most, if not all, relate to change.

Most adults are afraid of change. We are creatures of habit, and we like for things to be predictable and orderly. This sameness carries throughout every part of our lives, and is demonstrated by the things we do every day. Each day when we go to work, do we go a different way from the day before? No, unless a wreck or road construction detours us, or we are spies for a foreign government and fearful for our lives do we ever change our route to work. We go the same way every day.

When you go to church, do you sit in a different place each week? No, unless someone else beats you to your place, or there is a leak in the roof dripping down on your seat. You sit in the same vicinity in the church week after week. My pastor tells me that he can just about tell who is not at church each week by looking through the congregation and seeing which people are not in their normal places.

We go to bed about the same time every night and get up the next morning within a few minutes of the time we got up the day before. We eat at roughly the same times every day. We go through the same procedure to get dressed and ready in the mornings no matter what we wear. We know what time we have to leave for work each day to get us there on time and know when we will be home in the afternoon. Think about it. Just about everything we do is a repeat of something we did the day before. We like things to be the same and at times will avoid change at all cost. Unfortunately, when we consciously fight change, we unconsciously quit learning.

In contrast to adults, when you were a child you were constantly learning. Just as you did, children work hard at learning everything they can each day. Their success at growing up and maturing depends on their ability to learn everything they can as fast as possible.

They learn from everyone and everything they come in contact with. They don't dismiss any new idea as trivial. It doesn't matter if this information is applicable to them at the time or not. They just absorb it and learn what they can from it.

Most adults are just the opposite. We accept everything and everyone with a grain of salt. We scrutinize every new idea, and if it's not applicable to us, we discard it as quickly as we get it.

In some cases, adults just plain ignore new ideas. We rarely allow new ideas to enter into our minds or be developed. We are afraid of what we might learn and how it might change us. We block it out. We turn it off. We stop it before it begins.

To be successful at anything you can never stop learning. You can never be satisfied with just what you know but must learn everything you can. You must grow each day, learning as you go. You can never dismiss or discard any new idea but must learn whatever you can from it.

If someone asks you to take on a new task at work, take a shot at it. It may not have a thing to do with your current job, but it will give you knowledge about another part of the business and may better clarify something you do now. At the least, it will give you another skill that may give you an advantage over someone else when it comes time for promotions or layoffs.

Be daring and take a different route to work tomorrow. You will be surprised at the things you will learn along the way. You will see interesting businesses and restaurants that you didn't know existed. You may see a gym that you may have been thinking about joining. You may find a park where you can take your family on picnics. Who knows, you may even find a better way to work.

If you really want to have some fun, sit in a different place each week in church. This will drive your pastor crazy. Best of all, you will meet and get to know new people. You never know when one of these people may be able to help you reach your next goal.

And sometimes, just like Jonathan, you will have to break things to find out what makes them tick. You may have to tear things apart piece by piece to truly understand their inner workings. You will have to look at and feel each part to know how it works with every other part. Your curiosity must drive you to learn and grow in knowledge. Knowledge is one of the most powerful tools you have. Use it to your advantage. Grow in knowledge, for knowledge will make you successful.

Children Learn from Their Mistakes

Mistakes come in all sizes. Some are an obstacle to your success and some are not. One thing is for sure, how you react to your mistakes will determine the impact they will have on you. Those who accept mistakes as a part of the growing process will succeed more easily. Those who look at every mistake as a setback will have difficulty being successful at anything.

There are four basic types of mistakes. We all know about the first type. I call it the "Embarrass Me Until It Hurts" type of mistake. You take your spouse to an expensive restaurant to have dinner. As you talk, the music is softly playing in the background. The waiter is not intrusive but helpful and available whenever you need him. The food is wonderful, and everything is going perfect.

Then it happens! About half way through the meal, you make the ultimate mistake. As you take a bite of your steak, it accidentally falls off the fork and slides down your favorite shirt into your lap. The steak sauce is all over the front of your shirt. The waiter tries to help, but the sauce smears and leaves a bigger stain than before.

The rest of the evening, you try to forget the stain on your shirt, but you can't. The once stimulating conversation has degraded to an occasional whisper. You convince yourself that the woman laughing uncontrollably at the next table is laughing at you. Your only thoughts are of removing yourself from the embarrassing situation and leaving the restaurant as quickly as possible.

As you leave the restaurant, the maitre d', trying to do his job, asks you if everything was okay. Without responding, you smile and leave as quickly as possible, trying to hide the stain on your shirt. There is nothing like the embarrassment of walking past the maitre d' of the most expensive restaurant in town wearing your meal.

This is an example of a simple, harmless mistake that rarely hurts anyone. We've all done it. We are so involved in the moment that we forget to lean over our plate to avoid dropping food on ourselves. It's a careless group of mistakes that occur in life that we must deal with on an almost daily basis. For some people it will totally ruin the evening. For others, it will provide a good laugh for all to enjoy.

The second type of mistake is similar to the first, but with a slight twist. I call it the "Oops, I'm Sorry" type of mistake. With this type of mistake, we do everything right, but something outside our control has changed to cause our action to be wrong.

This type of mistake disrupted my family's life several years ago when we built a new house. We decided that it might be a good idea to have an unlisted phone number, so we acquired a new number. It would provide us a measure of privacy and help control the interruptions during our family time. Well, it sounded like a good idea on paper anyway.

The first day we were living in the house, we received three wrong-number calls for the same person. "Is Ms. Weeks there?" the caller asked. In quick fashion we deduced that Ms. Weeks must have owned our telephone number before we did. For the next several weeks, we continued to get four to five calls a day for her.

For whatever reason, she had changed her number. She had obviously not told the countless number of people who called her on a regular basis. As a result, my family got to talk to all these lovely people on a daily basis. We called the telephone company to get her new number so we could pass it along to her friends when they called, but as you might imagine, she had an unlisted number, and the telephone company would not release it.

A painfully simple mistake that was no fault of the caller; they didn't know Ms. Weeks changed her telephone number. They called the same number they had always called. Something outside their control had changed and caused the number where they previously had reached her to be wrong. So much for my family's privacy!

After being in the house for three months, the daily calls started to subside. You would think by the first few days that all the people who called her on a regular basis would know she didn't have that number any more. Even today we still get an occasional call for her. By the way, if you are one of those callers that continue to call us, Ms. Weeks has changed her number!

The third type of mistake is different from the first two and requires a conscience effort. This mistake falls into the "I Told You So" group of mistakes and provides the best opportunity for learning. With this mistake, you know the pending action is a mistake, but you do it any way.

In 1986, we lived in Franklin, Kentucky, a little known town just north of the Tennessee state line. When I say little, I mean little. Our first day there one of the local residents told us, "Chances are you will never be mugged, but if you are, you will know who did it." We found this to be true.

About our second year there, my wife and I decided to plant a garden. Now, you would think that growing up in Alabama would have provided us a good background for that type of activity, but it didn't. That winter, we collected books on the subject and spent countless hours reading about what would grow in our climate and when to plant.

One Saturday morning I pulled out my recently purchased tiller and began to break the ground—just like the book said. Jonathan, who was about three at the time, followed me around like a little puppy dog. He was so intrigued by a machine that could break up the ground with such ease. He would sit on his haunches like an old farmer working in the fields and observe the activity from every possible angle.

Occasionally I would have to stop, and at those times, when the engine was not running, Jonathan would run up and get as close as possible. Just like everything else, he was so interested in how the equipment worked and would ask question after question. His little finger would point at the different parts with wonderful curiosity. Each time I would remind him that the tiller was very hot, and he shouldn't touch it. For several hours, Jonathan and I played that game. He would follow and watch, and when the tiller stopped, he would run up, point, and ask questions.

When I finished the job, we put the tiller away together. He continued to ask questions and to point at the different parts. Once again I reminded him that the tiller was very hot, and if he touched it, he would hurt himself. I'm sure by now you know where this story is going, but try not to get ahead of me.

On my way back to the house I heard a loud scream coming from behind me. In a split second, Jonathan had left my side without my knowledge and gone back into the shed. His curiosity had overtaken him, and he had grabbed the hot muffler. I don't know for sure, but perhaps that was his first move in an attempt to take it apart. However, the burning sensation from the hot muffler quickly changed his mind, and he let out a terrifying scream.

He knew the tiller was hot. I must have told him a hundred times in those last few hours. For whatever reason, Jonathan took it upon himself to touch it anyway.

As I rushed back into the shed, Jonathan was standing holding his little burnt hand outstretched toward me. Elephant sized tears streamed down his cheeks. It took everything I had to keep from saying I told you so, but I didn't.

For the rest of the night, my wife and I took shifts holding his hand in cold water to ease the pain. As soon as his hand would come out of the cold water, he would immediately begin to cry. He would look at his hand and say, "hot!"

From that moment on, until this day, if you tell Jonathan something is hot, he moves away from it instantly. As an older child, he would make a three-foot circle around anything he perceived as hot. Even at the age of twelve, he refused to remove his pizza from the hot oven.

I told Jonathan the tiller was hot. I told him repeatedly not to touch it, but he did anyway. What a wonderful learning experience! Don't get me wrong; it nearly broke my heart to see Jonathan in so much pain, but from that day forward, he knew what hot meant. To no avail, he was told repeatedly that touching the hot tiller would be a mistake. Not until he touched the muffler and experienced the pain that was a direct result of his mistake, did he learn and take corrective action to keep it from happening again.

The last type of mistake occurs when you know what you are about to do is a mistake, but you do it any way. I call it the "Knock Me Down Again" type of mistake. This is not the first time you have made this mistake. It was a mistake when you did it before, and you know it will be a mistake if you do it again, but you do it anyway.

It's hard to imagine anyone in his or her right mind making this mistake, but it happens all the time. People go out and have too much to drink. They spend the rest of the night hugging the toilet. They are sicker than they ever thought possible. They repeatedly say, "I'm never going to do this again!" but they do. Within a short period of time, they do it again.

When it comes to this type of mistake, food is my downfall. I love to eat. And at times, I love to overeat. Sometimes I will eat until I make myself sick.

Now, I know if I overeat, I will get sick. It has happened to me many times before. Even as I am overeating, I know that what I am doing is a mistake, but I do it anyway.

Most repetitive mistakes such as these are a result of compulsive behavior. We know that what we are about to do is wrong, but we do it anyway. The severity and frequency of the mistakes we make will determine the obstacles we must overcome to be successful. With hard work and dedication, we can bring these types of mistakes under control.

All four types of mistakes are a part of life. It is a part of growing and learning. How we react to each mistake in life determines how successful we will be.

Children make lots of mistakes. Each mistake is a new experience. Every time they fall down, every time they say something they shouldn't, and every time they touch something that hurts them, they learn a little something about themselves and the world around them. They don't worry about making mistakes. They just pick themselves up and move on. This is their process of learning, and through their mistakes, they grow to become adults.

Adults look at mistakes differently. Instead of using each mistake as a learning experience, we let mistakes control our lives and defeat us. Some of us feel sorry for ourselves and think that our problems are greater than anyone else's are. Instead of correcting our mistakes and moving on with our lives like children do, we have a tendency to repeat them over and over.

Unfortunately, adults, just like children, must sometimes be burned before they learn from their mistakes. Not until they feel pain, as was in Jonathan's case, do they learn to take action to prevent them from happening again.

Making mistakes is good. Nothing worthwhile has ever been accomplished without making mistakes and learning from them. And yes, some mistakes lead to failure, but that's okay, too.

If you are making mistakes, you are doing. A person who never makes mistakes isn't doing anything. If you are not doing, you will not succeed no matter how much you want to.

Don't be afraid of mistakes, but cherish them for the knowledge they give you. Just like Jonathan, you could hear a hundred times that you are about to make a mistake, but only when you experience the mistake first hand will you ever truly learn the power of it.

Now, I'm not suggesting you go out and burn yourself to experience the power of learning from your mistakes. But sometimes it takes getting burned before we reevaluate our actions and take corrective measures.

The main idea is that you learn from your mistakes. Take the knowledge you have received from the mistake, and then take corrective action to keep it from reoccurring. As I said before, making mistakes is good. However, not taking action to prevent them from happening repeatedly will always hinder you from reaching your full potential.

Mistakes like the first two types—"Embarrass Me Until It Hurts" and "Oops, I'm Sorry"—are almost uncontrollable. They are going to happen no matter what you do. Dropping food on yourself or accidentally calling the wrong number is going to happen from time to time. Most mistakes of this nature are harmless and should be treated as such.

Unfortunately, occasionally mistakes are destructive. For example, you get distracted while driving your car and have a wreck—a careless mistake leading to a destructive action. Obviously, you should have been paying more attention to your driving, but mistakes like these are going to happen, and you can't do much to prevent them. Accept them for the careless acts they are, move on with your life, and pay closer attention next time.

The third type of mistake—"I Told You So"—is a true learning experience and should be cherished. There will always be people telling you that what you are about to do is a mistake. At times you will experience ridicule, contempt, and isolation, but unless you are willing to take a chance, you will never experience the learning power of a mistake.

In Jonathan's case, I told him several times that the tiller was hot and that if he touched it, he would hurt himself. But Jonathan didn't listen to my warnings. I can only speculate that his only concern was to examine the tiller to determine how it worked. Did Jonathan make a mistake when he didn't listen to me? Yes, he burned his hand and spent most of night with his hand in a bowl of cold water. Did he learn a valuable lesson from his mistake? You bet he did! He learned that if he touched something hot, it was going to burn him, and getting burned was no fun. Would Jonathan have learned the same lesson if he had taken my advice and not touched the tiller? Yes and no. Not until the consequences of his action caused him pain, which overruled his inquisitiveness and stopped his course of action, did he truly understand the meaning of hot. From that moment forward, when I said something was hot to Jonathan, I got his complete attention.

Like children, adults learn best by doing, by making mistakes, and by learning from the consequences of their mistakes. If you are not making mistakes, you are not doing. If you are not doing and making mistakes, you are not learning. To be successful, you must never fear making a mistake, but you must learn all you can from them when they happen.

The fourth type of mistake—"Knock Me Down Again"—is a repetitive mistake that compulsive behaviors sometimes cause. Anyone who knowingly makes mistakes repeatedly will always have difficulty succeeding. Seek professional help if necessary to break the trend. Don't be one of these people!

By the way, our garden was a mistake as well; all that reading and planning did very little to make us successful. Our garden was a complete failure the first year. It did not begin to flourish until following years, when we had made enough mistakes and had time to learn from them.

Enjoy your mistakes the way you did when you were a child. Don't look at mistakes negatively, but look at mistakes as vehicles of learning that will carry you down the quickest road to success. Like an artist, incorporate your mistakes into your work. An artist never worries about a mis-stroke in his or her painting, but incorporates it into the painting to strengthen the final work—so must you.

I have a rule about mistakes that I have told every person who has ever worked for me. If people won't remember your mistake in one hundred years, or if your mistake doesn't rewrite history, don't worry about it! Correct your mistake, use it as a learning experience, and get back to work. Now, go make mistakes, and have fun!

Children Learn from Other Successful People

Because of the separation of ages between my sister and myself and my wife and her brother—six years to be exact—we decided to have our children much closer together. We felt that it was important to have them as close together as possible so that they could grow up and, hopefully, through their similar experiences, be closer to each other in the end. With this in mind, we had our children two years apart.

During this time my wife worked out of our home. She is a music teacher by profession and taught piano lessons privately. It was the perfect arrangement. She was able to work doing what she loved and at the same time, she was able to stay home with the kids. My wife and I felt it was important that she stay home with our children during their early years.

For a three-year period, she did exactly that. She stayed at home with our children catering to their every need. While she taught lessons, one of my wife's older students played with the children in the next room. She could teach her piano lessons, but if needed, she was close by to help.

It was an ideal situation for me, as well. Our home was about five miles from my job and allowed me to come home for lunch each day. As I said earlier, lunchtime was a special time for me. Each day my entire family would sit around the table and discuss the day while we ate. Of course, it was a challenge at times to talk with my children while they learned the English language, but we had fun trying, and at the time, that's all that mattered.

Kristen was eleven months old when we moved to Louisville, Kentucky. My wife decided to return to the workforce and began teaching in one of the local school systems. It was an apprehensive time for both of us when we had to place both our children in a daycare.

We visited several daycares before we found one that we were both comfortable with. The first few weeks were very traumatic for everyone. Both children were not happy being left with total strangers. Each morning the workers distracted our children as my wife quickly slipped out the door. It wasn't a pretty sight. My children screamed. My wife cried. I wasn't sure what to do. For the first time since their birth, my children were separated from their mother.

As time went by, things did get better. My children stopped screaming, and my wife quit sneaking out of the building. Unfortunately, it took my wife a little longer to stop crying than it did for my children to stop screaming, but she eventually did, and things improved daily.

At first my children were so happy to see us when we arrived at the daycare center to pick them up. They would drop whatever they were doing and run to the door to greet us. They would grab our hand and refuse to let go until we got into the car.

After a few weeks, they were standing in front of the window watching and waiting for us to arrive. I guess they recognized and learned the order in which parents picked up the other children. They knew that when Tommy's mom arrived, it was only a short time before we would be there to pick them up. As soon as they saw Tommy and his mom leave, they went to the window where they stood to watch and wait for one of us to arrive.

A few months went by, and the children we once had to distract to drop off, we now had to drag out the door to go home. They didn't want to leave. They wanted to stay and play with their new friends.

This is about the same time we began to notice a big change in our children. We were amazed at the new things they learned from one day to the next. Communication, coordination, and motor skills seemed to improve daily. We looked forward to picking them up each day to see the changes that had taken place.

We were equally amazed at how much quicker Kristen learned her basic skills than Jonathan did. She dressed herself at an earlier age than Jonathan did. She potty trained sooner than Jonathan did. She made complete sentences sooner than Jonathan did. She just seemed to learn things much quicker than Jonathan had.

My wife and I discussed this often. Was Kristen smarter than Jonathan was? Did she have better coordination that allowed her to pick up those skills more quickly? Was it because Kristen was a girl, and girls just matured faster than boys did? I don't think so. So what was the difference? Unlike Jonathan, other successful children surrounded Kristen during this time of her development—kids of all ages, at all skill levels, watching and teaching each other.

If you want to be successful, you have to surround your self with successful people. Children know this. They do it every day. Children naturally gravitate toward other children. They run, jump, and climb trees together. They play Barbie dolls and Power Rangers and imitate the actions of their parents. They watch each other and learn as they play. Their cooperative skills work together to form a basis of knowledge, sharing what they know and learning from each other.

The greatest exchange of knowledge happens when children are around other children. Children bring their own unique talents and skills to be demonstrated and shared with the group. Learning occurs when children with more advanced skills demonstrate their abilities, while children with lesser skills mimic or imitate their actions. This is a give and take exchange of knowledge—children teaching children.

Sometimes adults fail to realize the wealth of knowledge that surrounds them. We are so caught up in trying to do everything ourselves, we shut out and never use the resources that abound around us. Somehow, we believe that if we ask for help or advice, we look weak. Our pride gets in our way, and we refuse to solicit help from those who can help us the most.

Just as when you were a child, if you want to be successful as an adult, you have to learn from other successful people. You have to surround yourself with people who are already doing what you want to do. You must identify people around you whom you can learn from and will help you reach your dream. Is there someone you know who is already doing what you want to do? Is there someone where you work who can help you get to where you want to go? Is there anyone in your church or community who has skills you desire? Search out people that can help you realize your dreams and learn everything you can from them. They have already accomplished what you want to accomplish. They have already made many of the mistakes that you are destined to make. Take advantage of their experience and learn from their wisdom.

Children are like sponges. They watch, listen, and soak up everything they come in contact with—good and bad. They use all their senses, and they absorb and learn everything presented to them.

When Jonathan was between three and four, his favorite book was the Radio Shack catalog. Every night before bedtime, we would go through the catalog together. He would point to a picture in the book, and I would tell him what it was. If he wanted to know more than that, we would stop and talk; otherwise, we would move on to whatever his little finger pointed to.

Occasionally we would make a trip to our local Radio Shack store. As soon as we walked through the door, Jonathan would go from rack to rack pointing to and naming the items. It was quite a sight. A little boy going through the store as quickly as possible naming everything he saw.

Everyone who saw him was amazed. Store managers were speechless. Customers stopped what they were doing and watched. Everyone wanted to know how he was doing it. It was simple. Jonathan used my ability to read. He took advantage of a skill that I had and used it to learn something he wanted to know.

Jonathan couldn't read, but he knew I could. He learned the names of the parts by surrounding himself with people who could teach him what he wanted to know.

Kristen's favorite book was a picture book of animals. The book was two inches thick and had rows and rows of pictures of every animal. Long before Kristen could read, she insisted we sit for hours on end pointing to the pictures and making the sound each animal makes. She, too, was using our knowledge to learn everything she could about animals. Once she learned all the animals, she would sit in the middle of the floor by herself, going through the pictures and making the animal sounds. We could sometimes hear her at night making animal sounds from her bedroom when she should have been asleep. She loved that book!

As adults we sometimes refuse to use this simple way of learning. We are so afraid of asking others for help. We are embarrassed that we can't do it ourselves.

Don't be afraid to ask for help. If you want to start a landscaping service, find someone who is already doing it and learn from him or her. If you want to change jobs or start a new career, learn from other people who have done it. If you want to lose weight, learn from other people who have been successful losing weight. In short, whatever you want to accomplish, identify the people around you who can help you succeed. Surround yourself with their knowledge, and learn from their mistakes. It has been my experience that most people will be more than happy to help you.

Learn all you can from other successful people. Use this pool of knowledge and experience to propel yourself to wherever you want to go. Success can come to you through many means, but success will come to you more quickly by taking advantage of the successes of others. Success is all around you. Find it, and use it to your advantage.

Children, If They Don't Know, Will Ask Questions

Children never hesitate to ask why. They question everything. If there is something they want to know, they ask. If there is something they don't understand, they will ask question after question until they do.

Jonathan wanted to know how everything works. He would corner you for hours at a time asking questions relentlessly. Jonathan was a master of the word 'how'. How does this work? How does that work? How do they work together? He understood the power of the word and used it to his advantage. When he ran out of questions or if your answers didn't totally satisfy his quest for knowledge, he would tear whatever he didn't understand apart piece by piece to see how it worked.

Kristen on the other hand, was a master of the word 'why.' She was ruthless with this word and could literally wear you out using it.

"Kristen, please come here," I asked.

In her most innocent voice, she replied, "Why?"

Kristen always had to know why she was doing something. She really didn't care that much about how something worked. She was more concerned about the why than the how.

"Kristen, please sit in the chair."

"Why?"

"Kristen, please roll up your window."

"Why?"

"Why? Because I told you to," I demanded! Great answer, huh? Not really, but as adults, we sometimes respond harshly to children who do not accept our authority without question. We think, Kristen, how dare you question my authority! Who does she think she is? When I told her to do something, I expected her to do it without question! I'm her daddy, and when I said jump, I expected her to ask how high!

However, Kristen was not concerned about my authority level. She was only concerned about how my decision would affect her. She wasn't always convinced that my requests were in her best interest. Until she was convinced that they were, she would "why" me to death.

As I said before, Kristen had a habit of playing with her gum. She liked to stretch it out of her mouth with her thumb and first finger. Sometimes she would have several strands of gum stretched as far as her arm would reach. Just as it was about to bend and drop to the floor, she would quickly bite it back into her mouth.

"Kristen, please quit playing with your gum, and stop stretching it out of your mouth," I would say.

"Why?"

"Because your gum is intended to stay in your mouth," I would tell her.

"Why?"

"Because if you keep stretching your gum, you might get it in your hair, and then we will have to cut your beautiful hair to get it out."

"Why?"

"Because once you get gum in your hair, believe me, you can't get it out any other way."

"Why?"

"Because gum and hair don't mix," I said.

"Why?"

"Because if we don't cut it out, you will go around the rest of your life with gum stuck in your hair."

"Why?"

"Why? Because I told you to stop stretching your gum!"

Did she stop playing with her gum? No. I was never able to convince her that it was in her best interest.

Children are that way. If they want to know something, they will ask. If they don't think you've got their best interest in mind, they will question your authority until you convince them that you do. If there is something they don't understand or want to know about, they will not hold back from asking questions to satisfy their curiosity.

For whatever reason, adults sometimes hold back and never ask questions. We accept and are somehow satisfied with lame or half-hearted answers that people give us. Are we afraid to question someone's authority? Are we are afraid that someone might think our question is stupid or, worse yet, are afraid that our question might make people think less of us? Bottom-line, for whatever reason, we accept things as presented and rarely question or allow our curiosity to be satisfied. As a result, we never know. We never claim or use to our advantage the power of knowledge that comes from a question.

Children are not afraid to ask questions. They could care less whether they look stupid or not. If they don't understand, they ask because they want to know. They are never embarrassed by anything, and they will ask any question until they understand. Ask your parents. I guarantee you were the same way, too.

If you don't know or want to know something, ask. If you don't know how something works, ask someone to explain it to you. If you don't understand why something is happening, ask questions until you do. If you don't think someone is considering your best interest, ask why not.

Use questions to your advantage. Use the word 'how' to understand the inner-workings of how things operate. How does this process work? How would it function if we changed this part of the process? How can we meet and exceed our customer's needs? How can we treat our employees better? How do we handle this particular problem?

Use the word why to question the status quo. Why do we do it this way? Why didn't we try something else when we weren't happy with the way this was working? Why hasn't someone ever tried doing it this way? Why don't we discuss our ideas, and come up with a solution we can all live with?

Knowledge is power and a key component of success. How do you expect to be successful at something if you don't know everything about it or understand how it works? How can you feel assured that your best interest is in mind if you don't question those who are in authority?

Question everything. If you don't know, ask. If you don't ask, you will never know. And if you never know, success will be difficult. Success comes to those who question everything and are never satisfied until they know it all.

In summary, to be successful at everything you do, you must know everything you can. You can never stop learning new things. If you need to break something to understand how it works, then break it! Learn everything you can while you tear it apart.

Second, don't be afraid of making mistakes. Mistakes are great teachers of life. Learn everything you can about every mistake you make, and move on with your life with your newfound knowledge. Remember, if you are not making mistakes, you are not learning.

Third, if you need to accomplish something you know little about, surround yourself with other people who have the skills you need! Use their knowledge to help you do the things you need to do.

Finally, if you don't know something, ask! There are no stupid or inappropriate questions if there is something you need to know.

Never stop learning! There is a reason it is the fifth fundamental element of being successful at everything you do. Your success depends on your knowledge. Learn everything you can as you did when you were a child. The effort you took to gain knowledge when you were a child is the same effort you need to make to be successful as an adult.

Think Outside the Lines

To be successful at everything we do, we must be able to think outside the lines. Not allowing imaginary boundaries—that we occasionally draw around ourselves—is critical to finding solutions to problems that seem unsolvable. As in most cases in life, the only boundaries we really have are the limits we place on ourselves. When we remove these limits, success quickly follows. Therefore, thinking outside the lines is the sixth fundamental element of being successful and is the next building block of success.

When we look at empty two-liter bottles, we see empty bottles. We see plastic containers destined for disposal that once held our favorite drinks. Oh, we may look inside the bottle cap to see if we have won the current contest, but when we finish the drink, we can't wait to throw out the bottle to make room for the next one.

When children look at empty two-liter bottles, they see unlimited possibilities. They see a world of wonder waiting to tap into. They don't see bottles that have finished their usefulness, but bottles waiting to be shaped into something special. They watch the liquid levels, and when the bottles are empty, they claim them for themselves and hide them from the trash until they can use them.

Jonathan has always liked to build things. He has always been able to take the most insignificant items and make them into unforgettable things.

To Jonathan, an empty two-liter bottle is the basis of a thousand different projects, from a simple terrarium to an underwater breathing apparatus. Just like many children, he can't wait until a bottle is empty and ready for transformation. I cannot remember the times that my wife or I had thrown a bottle in the trash to only find it later in Jonathan's room.

Jonathan's most memorable bottle project came when he decided to make a device that would allow him to breathe under water. Just like the air tanks professional divers use, he was convinced that with the addition of a few other parts, he could use the bottle to stay under water for extended periods. In his mind he visualized the final product to determine what parts he needed and how they should fit together.

I can just imagine the dreams he must have had when he looked at that empty bottle—dreams of exploring shipwrecks, diving for gold doubloons, or hunting for sharks in the ocean; dreams that only hard work and an empty bottle could fulfill.

For several hours Jonathan collected the items he needed to build his project. He went through his boxes of parts from previously dismantled toys. He looked through kitchen cabinets and the refrigerator in hopes of finding anything he could empty into something else and reuse. He looked through the family toolbox for spare items that might fit his requirements. He described mental images of items he needed to other family members in hopes that they could provide him with these essential parts. When Jonathan had collected all the parts he needed, he piled them on the floor to begin work.

To the untrained eye of an adult, this pile of parts didn't look like much—a couple of two-liter bottles, two rubber hoses, a medical "Y" valve he got from his granny (a nurse), a roll of duct tape, and a hot glue gun. But to Jonathan's trained eye, these parts represented the beginning of an adventure.

Jonathan spent the next few days building, testing, and refining his breathing device. It looked similar to a tank that any scuba diver would use. It had two empty two-liter bottles taped together sided by side with duct tape. Coming out of the mouth of each bottle was a rubber hose glued into place with about three inches of hot melt glue to form a tight seal. The other end of each hose connected to each side of the "Y" connector, forming a crude mouthpiece. It wasn't much to look at, but it held the hopes and dreams of a small child who dared to imagine.

The time he spent testing his device was especially interesting. Every night at bath time, Jonathan would head to the bathroom, fill the tub up as deep as he could, and climb in with his breathing device. I have never seen him before or since so anxious to take a bath. For hours at a time, he played in the water testing his device, making small adjustments, and testing again. By the time we got him out of the tub each night, his water was ice cold. He was so wrinkled he looked like a little old man.

You are probably wondering if we were worried Jonathan would drown in our bathtub. We did worry a little, but we watched him closely and never let him do anything dangerous. It was an important time for Jonathan. He believed in what he was doing, and we saw no reason to keep him from chasing his dream.

The final and ultimate test came when we traveled to Alabama to visit family. My parents have a swimming pool that Jonathan was determined to go diving in. He was certain his device would allow him to stay under water for hours at a time.

As we packed the car to leave, Jonathan's only interest was his breathing device. Normally we had to pack half his room before we could leave. He was never quite sure what he might need while he was gone, but this time he only had one purpose in mind. I guess he figured he would only have time for one thing, and that was all that he packed.

Well, after days of waiting, the big day finally came. Of course, Jonathan, with his device in hand, was the first one to the pool. He stood at the side of the pool waiting for the rest of us to come out of the house. Within a few minutes, we all stood with him as he tied his device on his back with a piece of string.

With the bottles on his back, the "Y" connector in his mouth, and borrowed goggles from his cousin, he made his first dive. We all stood close by with emergency rescue thoughts on our minds. As soon as he went down, he came up. The bottles acted like huge floats on his back and brought him quickly up to the surface.

With a minor adjustment, he moved the bottles from his back to his chest and tried again. This time he stayed down longer. He didn't set any records, but he quickly proved his device worked. Even though the longest he ever stayed down was a few seconds, he felt he could have stayed down longer. Jonathan felt that if we had only allowed him to weigh himself down so that he couldn't float back up to the surface, he could have stayed under water indefinitely. Unfortunately for Jonathan, that was one idea my wife and I were not willing to let him try.

So what does all of this mean? It demonstrates how children think outside the lines. To you or me, the bottles were empty and had little or no value. They only took up space that could be used for other things. The sooner we rid ourselves of them, the better.

Children are just the opposite. They look at the bottles and visualize what they could become. The bottles, now that they are empty, have more value than before. They think outside the lines and create opportunities to satisfy their dreams.

When you were a child, did you ever take things lying around the house and make them into something special? Sure you did. We all made wonderful things from insignificant items. That's what children do. That's what you did. That's what I did. As children, we easily stepped outside the lines of normal thinking to chase our dreams. This kind of thinking is what made you successful as a child, and it will make you successful as an adult, too.

Why do adults have trouble thinking outside the lines? Why do they allow boundaries to hold them captive and prevent them from conquering the many opportunities around them? I think their problems start from the moment they hold crayons in their hands and color their first pictures.

Coloring pictures is a fun activity. Kids of all ages love to color and, if allowed, will color for hours at a time. By picking just the right color—out of a 1001-count crayon box—and applying it in just the right spots, they make the picture come alive. Their imaginations run rampant to satisfy their creativity and to produce something beautiful.

Then it happens. They get their first instruction in the art of coloring. "No honey! You need to stay inside the lines," a well-meaning adult instructs them. From that moment forward, they never look at lines or boundaries the same way. We program them to think going outside the lines is not acceptable, and that it lessens the value of their creativity. That line of reasoning continues throughout childhood.

As children get a little older, how they dress becomes an issue. Boundaries are drawn around them that are linked to acceptance. Here are just a few examples:

- Socks must match and be the same color.
- Plaids and stripes don't go together.
- Shirt and pants (blouse and skirt) must color coordinate.
- Shoes must be tied at all times.
- Sunday clothes, school clothes, and play clothes shall never meet.
- Clean underwear must be worn whenever they leave the house.

It doesn't stop there. They sign up for Little League Baseball, and they must stay within other lines and boundaries that besiege them. See if you recognize any of these:

- Choke up on the bat after two strikes.
- Batter should always take the pitch on a three balls and no-strike count.
- Pitcher should never throw a strike with a no balls and two-strike count.
- Left-handers play first base and right field.
- Best infielder always plays shortstop. Worst infielder plays second base.
- Best outfielder always plays center field. Worst outfielder plays right field.
- The person with the best throwing arm always plays third base. Worst usually plays second base.
- The person who can catch the best plays the catcher position. Second best catcher plays first base.

The list could go on and on. Everywhere children turn, people establish lines and create boundaries around them, teaching them that staying inside the lines is the norm and that going outside the lines is unsatisfactory. By the time they reach adulthood, these messages are deeply rooted in their minds and can influence every decision they make.

As adults, even though these lines may influence our decisions, we may not recognize them as boundaries when we see them. We block them from our conscience minds and pretend they are not there. Somehow, our unconscious minds remind us of the unacceptable consequences of crossing the lines. What happens when we realize the consequences of crossing the lines? We back off, and although we may not be comfortable or happy with the outcomes, we accept the false security and protection of staying inside the lines.

We weren't that way as children. Did you ever let someone keep you from doing something you wanted to do? Children have no lines or boundaries. They only begin to have boundaries when adults draw lines around them. Children react differently than adults to the lines adults place around them. Unlike adults, children know exactly where every line is. They acknowledge those lines and are not afraid to cross them. They never let lines or boundaries keep them from doing what they think is right. They never let lines keep them from making things better. Children never let lines or boundaries keep them from doing things they want to do.

When Jonathan looked at the empty two-liter bottle, he thought outside the lines and saw something that wasn't there. He didn't see an empty bottle. He saw a tank filled with air. He envisioned hoses running from the tank to his mouth that would allow him to breathe the air inside the tank. He dreamt of himself with the tank strapped to his back swimming under water.

The safe thing for Jonathan to do would have been for him to stay inside the lines and accept the bottle for what it was – an empty bottle; a bottle that had reached its useful life and was bound for disposal. Instead, Jonathan looked at the empty bottle, crossed the lines of traditional and accepted thinking, and created a device that allowed him to breathe under water for short periods of time.

It's not easy to think outside the lines. It's not easy to try new and different ideas. Jonathan took a chance when he took the bottle and dared to dream. He took a chance that his idea wouldn't work. He took a chance that people might not accept his idea and laugh at him. He took a chance that he might get hurt trying to breathe out of a two-liter bottle. But sometimes you have to take a chance. You have to think outside the lines to solve a difficult problem. You have to use ideas that have never been used before. Sometimes it will be necessary for you to step outside the lines to realize your dream.

Don't be afraid to think outside the lines. Don't be afraid to take a chance. Don't be afraid to knock down the boundaries that others place around you. Just as you did when you were a child, don't be afraid to cross the line.

To be successful at everything you do, you have to think outside the lines. You have to be able to recognize your boundaries and be willing to cross them within a moment's notice. To solve the difficult problems you have look past the obvious and traditional ways of thinking and visualize the untapped possibilities. Success is easy to those who can think outside the lines and see the opportunities on the other side.

Tell Everyone

Believe it or not, some people in this world want to help us be successful. Family, friends, colleagues, and sometimes even complete strangers are more than willing to help us achieve our goals. To provide them with opportunities to help us, we must tell them about our dreams. We must share what we want with anyone who will listen to us.

During my career I have developed several websites. Throughout this process I've learned several valuable lessons. Most importantly, for a website to increase its traffic and be successful, the content needs to be excellent, and you have to let people know about it any way you can. You have to buy advertising space. You have to connect with people on Facebook® and Twitter®. You have to put your web address on all your literature and business cards. You have to make videos for YouTube® to demonstrate your product or idea. You have to do everything you can do and tell everyone you can tell about your website. I wish I could remember who gave me this invaluable advice: "If you don't advertise your website and use every opportunity to tell everybody you can about it, it is like having a billboard in your basement—no one will ever see it. And if no one ever sees your website, it will never be successful."

This same advice can apply to our goals and dreams. We can't keep our goals and dreams a secret from those who can help us succeed. To increase our chances of being successful, we must tell everyone who will listen about what we want to do or accomplish. You never know who might be willing to help us get what we want. Telling everyone about your goals and dreams is the seventh and final fundamental element of being successful and the next building block of success.

From the moment Jonathan was born, he let everyone within screaming distance know when he wanted something. He didn't care who heard him; he would scream at the top of his lungs until we fulfilled his every need and desire. Even as he lay in the hospital nursery waiting to go home, he fine-tuned his persuasive skills. He quickly learned the power of his scream and about how to use it to get whatever he wanted.

The first night we brought him home from the hospital we, too, quickly learned the power of his scream. Every hour, on the hour, we could hear his high-pitched screech throughout our apartment. He quickly conditioned us to come running whenever he made that sound. Although he didn't always seem to know what he wanted when one of us got there, he kept us running just the same.

As time went by, Jonathan's screams became more distinctive and more recognizable. We no longer had to go through a list of possibilities and needs assessments to determine exactly what he wanted. Although subtle to the casual listener, his shrills became more identifiable and relatable to a specific need that he had. He developed a distinctive sound for each need and used it instinctively to let us know what he wanted.

As Jonathan got older and began to speak, we no longer had to listen for a distinctive scream, but he told us about his every want. This was a great improvement over our previous system. It not only kept us from going through a period of trial and error in which we tried to determine what he wanted, but it also allowed us to satisfy his needs much quicker. He told us what he wanted and we took care of it.

Of course, Jonathan's ability to speak added another dimension to his ability to tell us what he wanted. It was especially noticeable when we went shopping. As we went down every aisle, he was sure to tell us about at least twelve different things that he wanted. It didn't matter to him whether he needed it or not, he asked for it. It didn't matter to him if he didn't know what the item was or what it did. It didn't matter to him that we had told him two aisles back that he couldn't have it. If he wanted it, he asked for it. And if he didn't get it the first time he asked, he asked again.

After he had asked—what seemed like several hundred times—and was almost sure we wouldn't give in, he began to sneak items into the buggy when we weren't looking. When our backs were turned, his little hands would throw things over the side of the buggy as it sat unattended in the middle of the aisle. Most times we hadn't even known that he had done it until we were unloading the buggy at the checkout register. After my wife and I conferred and determined that neither of us had put the item in the buggy, Jonathan would ask for it again. "Please let me have it Momma! I want this more than anything," he would plead. Sometimes it worked and sometimes it didn't. Jonathan knew this was his last chance to get the item on this trip, and he played it for everything it was worth. We apologized to the clerks, but they seldom seemed surprised. They simply placed the item alongside other items stacked around the counter left by all the parents of children who preceded us that day—children just like Jonathan trying to get what they wanted.

If children want something, they will let you know about it. They don't hold back. They don't keep it a secret from anyone. If they want the newest video game that just hit the market, they ask for it. They don't care how much it costs or if they have the right game system to play it on. If they want it, they ask for it. If they want to stay up past their regular bedtime to finish watching a television show, they ask. They don't care if it is a school night and have to get up early the next morning. They just know that a great television show is on, and they want to see the rest of it.

Children are not afraid to ask for whatever they want and will use any opportunity do it. They will pull open your eyelid and wake you up from a deep sleep to ask if they can change the TV channel. They will interrupt you midsentence of a stimulating conversation with a friend to get you to tie their shoes. They will pull on your sleeve while you are talking on the phone to your boss to ask for a glass of milk. They will make out a seven-page list of toys they want for Christmas in August and update it monthly. They will open the shower door to tell you they want to answer the phone the next time it rings. They will tell you that they need to go to the bathroom really bad from across the room of an expensive restaurant. They will get out of the tub and walk naked into the living room where people from the local church are visiting for the first time to ask you to help them dry off. If children want something, nothing will stop them from telling you about it.

Children know instinctively if they don't ask for whatever they want, there is no way they will ever get it. They realize that whatever they want will never be handed to them on a platter. They know that if they want something, they have to let the people around them who can give it to them know about it. They reason with themselves, "What is the worst thing that can happen if I ask for something?" They answer, "The person asked could say no. Big deal!" They know they will never take no for an answer. They will use the *Equal Authority Slide*, *The Outsiders Shuffle,* or *The in Your Face* method to get whatever they want anyway. So, what does a child have to lose by telling? Nothing. Nothing at all!

Do you remember telling everyone what you wanted when you were a child? If you don't, I'll bet your parents remember. Ask them sometime. I'm sure they recall countless stories of you asking for whatever you wanted.

Why is it that when we move out of our childhood stage, we stop telling people what we want? Is it because we are afraid of what people might think about us? Are we afraid that others may laugh at or ridicule our ideas? Are we afraid that people will discount our ideas and tell us we are wasting our time? Not to say that this won't happen, but for all those who may be negative toward you, many more will want to help you travel down your path to success.

Just like children, adults have nothing to lose either. Adults have nothing to lose by telling people what they want. If you want something, you not only have to work hard for it, but you have to ask for it as well. No one will ever hand it to you on a platter. You have to let people know what you want, and allow them to help you get it.

It could be anything, but let's say there is a job in your company you really want. As far as you are concerned, the job is perfect for you. You like everything about it and are willing to do anything to get it. What do you do? Do you privately wish to yourself and keep your fingers crossed hoping someone will ask you to do the job someday? Do you hope that the person in the position now will be hit by a bus and create a job opening? Do you go to a fortuneteller and ask that person to read your future as it relates to the job? I hope not!

So what do you do? You tell everybody who could potentially help you get that job. You tell everybody who will listen to you that you want that job more than anything. You go to your boss and tell him. You go to the boss over the position you want and tell him. You tell his boss and his boss's supervisor. You tell everybody in the department where the job opening is located. And if the custodian will listen, you tell him or her, too. You don't stop until you tell everyone who might be able to help you get the job.

Let's say you want to start your own business. You have a great idea that the world is waiting for you to develop. Your career is going nowhere and you are ready to make a change, but you need startup capital. What do you do? Do you wait for someone with a similar idea to approach you to start a business? Do you play the lottery, believing that someday you will have the winning ticket that will provide you with the funds you need to start your business? Do you sit back and do nothing, hoping that when your "someday" comes, no one will have used your idea ahead of you? Of course you don't!

So what do you do? You tell your banker about your idea. He or she may not give you any money, but could give you invaluable advice. You tell your relatives. Who knows, Aunt Mary might have just come into a lot of money that she is willing to lend you. You tell your friends and their friends. Who knows, someone they know might be looking for a business just like yours to invest in. You tell acquaintances and complete strangers too. Who knows what they might be willing to share with you. Take every opportunity to tell someone about your idea or dream.

So, why do you tell everyone? Why, because you never know who can help you. You never know who knows someone that you need to meet. You never know who has information that could help you get a foot up on the competition or who might have an insight about your dream. You never know who might be friends with someone willing to put in a good word for you. You never know who talks to who that might have a stake or a voice in something you need. You never know who is related to whom and who might be willing to make you a part of the family. You never know who has already done what you want to do and could tell you what it takes to do it. You just never know who could help you until you tell your wants and dreams to those around you.

Now, I'm not saying that everyone you talk to will help you. Some will not even be willing to listen. Some will make fun of you and try to discourage you from going after your dream. Some will feel they are in competition with you and will talk against you every chance they get. Some will tell you they will help you and never do the first thing. Don't be discouraged!

I'm also not saying that everyone you talk with will help you right away. It may take months of talking to some people before they will offer to help. It may take weeks for someone to talk to someone else on your behalf. It might take some time for someone to remember a friend or a contact that can help you. You may have to talk to some people repeatedly before they will do anything. Be persistent and never give up.

It's like a farmer planting a seed. Like the farmer, you have to plant the seed, and then sit back and let it grow. From experience you know you have to plant many seeds knowing that some will do well and provide you with much fruit, while others will wither and die. You have to tend to the fields every day, not spending too much time with each plant but working to keep the weeds and thorns from choking them all out. With time, the seeds grow into healthy plants, providing you with food for the harvest.

Children know this. They may not be able to explain it, but they know that to get what they want they have to tell everybody. They know that telling more people increases their odds of getting what they want. Jonathan knew that to increase his odds, he had to tell everybody. So he did. He told his parents, grandparents, relatives, neighbors, and even complete strangers every time he wanted something. My parents tell me that when I was a child, I would call my grandparents in the middle of the night asking for a toy my parents had refused to get me earlier in the day. Did I compel my grandparents to leave their house in the middle of the night to get me the toy? You bet I did!

As mentioned before, many people are out there waiting and willing to help you get what you want. If you want to be successful and get the help that you will sometimes need to follow your dream, you have to tell everybody about your wants and desires. Avoid holding back or keeping secrets from anyone. Plant your seed or idea in their minds, sit back, and allow it to grow and flourish. You have to make your dreams come alive in their minds, knowing that someday, someone will take action on your behalf.

One word of caution: be careful what you ask for. Make sure that what you ask for is what you really want. Why? Because whatever you ask for, you may just get.

You know it's funny. As Kristen grew up and began shopping with us, we thought things would be different with her. We thought that through the experience we gained with Jonathan, she would act much differently when we went shopping, but we were wrong. She, like Jonathan, threw items into the buggy when our backs were turned just as he had done. Just like Jonathan, she begged us for things all the way out the door to the car. Just as we had done with Jonathan, we left items at the checkout counter that had mysteriously appeared in our buggy.

The next time you are standing in line waiting to check out and see items stacked around the register, smile and remember that to be successful, you have to tell everyone about your goals and aspirations. You never know who can help you until you ask them. Those who tell the most will reap the greatest rewards from those who are waiting to help. Tell everybody, and enjoy the successes you receive.

Three Keys to Simplifying Success

Now that we have reviewed the seven fundamental elements of the building blocks of success, three additional things will simplify your journey, make success come easily to you, and make your journey enjoyable: have fun doing everything you do, use power phrases whenever possible, and keep a special friend close by your side. You will find that as you follow your goals and dreams these three things will become invaluable to simplifying your journey and allowing success to come more easily to you. Let's look at each one briefly.

Have Fun Doing Everything You Do

As I write this, I am sitting in my beach chair thinking back about how my little girl, Kristen, played in the sand during her first trip to the beach. We were on a family vacation in Myrtle Beach, South Carolina. It was a long-awaited vacation for our family to get away from the daily routine and enjoy each other's company for a few days.

My wife and I had always made a concerted effort to spend more time as a family and go places with our children. We realized their time with us was short, and before long, they would move in their own directions as they got older and their schedules got more complicated.

As I remembered Kristen playing in the sand, it reminded me of her first Christmas. My wife and I had searched for months for the right gifts. We wanted everything to be just right. We wanted Christmas morning to be a special day that Kristen would remember for the rest of her life.

As each day passed, our excitement grew, and by Christmas Eve, we had choreographed the following morning in our minds. We stayed up most of the night laying out the gifts under the tree in just the right places. We set up the video camera at just the right angle to catch every detail for posterity. We replayed over and over to each other the order in which we would allow her to open her gifts. It was her first Christmas, and we wanted everything to be just right.

As we lay in bed anticipating morning, we slept very little while we second-guessed our selection of gifts. Did we get the right things? Did we buy something she would like? What if she didn't like something? Do we take it back and exchange it for something else? After all, this is her first Christmas.

Christmas morning finally arrived, and we stood hovering over her bed while she slept. Her little body was sound asleep, not realizing the joy that awaited her. Should we wake her up? What if her brother Jonathan wakes up before she does? Will he be willing to wait until she wakes up so that we can open gifts as a family? For the next few minutes, we quietly paced back and forth in front of her bed, all the time hoping she would wake up. She didn't.

As we stood in her room, I saw Jonathan out of the corner of my eye dart past Kristen's door with wild abandonment, heading for the Christmas tree. In one giant leap—a leap only Superman could appreciate—I grabbed Jonathan by the arm and quickly moved him away from the tree. "Are you hungry son? How about we get something to eat before we open the gifts? Why, you can't open gifts on an empty stomach," I said while stalling for time. But my time had run out. He wasn't about to wait. We had to make a decision.

With reluctance, we woke Kristen up and took her to the living room, where we had neatly arranged all the presents. We justified our actions by rationalizing that we couldn't let her sleep her day away—not this day. This was her first Christmas.

She rubbed her eyes as we sat her down in front of the Christmas tree. As her eyes began to focus, an enormous smile appeared on her face. Her head quickly looked around the room as she surveyed the gifts. The look on her face said it all.

It was a proud moment for my wife and me. Months of planning had paid off, and as we all sat around the tree enjoying each other's company and the anticipation of the moment, everything was just right.

We sat Kristen's first gift in front of her as we had planned. Her little arms stretched out as far as they could reach for the package. For the first few seconds she threw her hands into the air as she laughed out loud and screamed with delight.

In a New York second—if there is such a thing—Kristen ripped the package open to reveal the contents. It was a beautiful doll. It had blond hair and blue eyes, with a cute little pink dress and white shoes. My wife and I had looked at about a hundred dolls before making a decision. The doll reminded us of Kristen, and although there were many others to choose from, we came back to this one repeatedly.

As quickly as Kristen picked up the doll, she sat it to the side. She immediately went back to the wrapping paper and found the bow. She didn't care about the doll. She didn't care that her mother and I searched for months for just the right doll. She only cared about the pretty bow that had caught her eye. That's what was important to her.

Every other package was the same. She only played with the wrapping paper and the bows. None of the real gifts interested her. To her, the packaging was the best gift she had gotten that Christmas. After some reflection, I agree. The intended gifts were insignificant to the meaning of Christmas or to her happiness.

The same excitement for wrapping paper and bows carried forward for years to come. By her first birthday, Kristen went from sleeping all the time to never sleeping. She lived every day to its fullest, as she spent every waking moment playing and learning. She was so afraid she would miss something that she never slept. She would go from one thing to the next with the same excitement I saw that first Christmas morning. Life was a big playground to Kristen, and she planned to play on everything.

As mentioned before, my job allowed me to come home for lunch. I looked forward to this special time every day. Her excitement about life recharged my batteries and gave me energy to carry back to work.

Each day during lunch, as we sat across the table from each other, we talked as best we could. Kristen talked to me nonstop in her one-year-old lingo while I listened intently trying to decipher her exact meaning. It didn't matter if we didn't exactly understand everything each other said; we understood enough.

Occasionally, Kristen's chatter would stop. In a split second, she would stop talking mid-sentence, or at least what I thought was mid-sentence, and a blank look would come over her face. Her eyes would begin to slowly close—first one eye and then the other. Her head would slowly droop forward, and just before her chin touched her chest, she would abruptly catch herself, jerk her eyes open, and wake herself up. For the next few moments, she would stare at me with a confused look on her face. She looked as if she were trying to determine who was talking—not wanting to interrupt if it wasn't her turn. As quickly as she had stopped talking, she started again.

This went on for several minutes. We would talk a little. Her head would bob a little. We would talk a little more, until finally, all talking stopped.

While looking across the table at Kristen, her eyes began to close once again. Her head slowly sank as before. Just as she should have caught herself and resumed our discussion, her head quickly plunged toward her plate. I jumped up from my chair to catch her head, but it was too late. Her face landed right in the middle of her mashed potatoes, her favorite food. Her head acted like someone had dropped it from a three-story building. Once it started to fall, I could do nothing to stop it. Gravity was going to run its course. And it did.

I quickly ran around the table and lifted Kristen's head out of her potatoes. As I pulled her head out of her plate, I could only imagine the headlines in the local newspaper: "*Girl Drowns in Mashed Potatoes While Her Father Watches from across the Table.*" With her eyes closed, potatoes covered her face as shaving cream covers a man's face in the morning—eyes still closed.

Lying on the counter only a few feet away was the towel I needed to wipe her face. Of course, those few feet might as well have been a mile. I couldn't reach the towel. I stretched one arm out as far as possible while holding her head out of the mashed potatoes with my other hand and could only get within inches of it. The only way to get it would be to let go of

Kristen's head. When I let go of her head to retrieve the towel, her head began to sink once again toward her plate.

For the next minute, I performed a famous Three Stooges routine. I would let go of her head, run toward the towel, and quickly return to Kristen to catch her head just before it hit her plate—never once getting the towel. Of course, if I were to get the towel, the inevitable had to happen. And it did. With the towel in hand, I once again picked Kristen's head up out of her plate and cleaned her face. She never woke up. Kristen played so hard from sunrise to bedtime that when her body had all it could take, she stopped wherever she was.

Even several years later while I watched her playing in the sand at the beach, she lived life to the fullest. She went from one thing to the next—wide open with only one purpose—having fun. You could say that playing was her profession.

To all children like Kristen, life is a playground. Theirs is a life dedicated to having fun! Sleeping very little, afraid to miss anything, going wide open from one thing to another just like a kid on a playground trying to play on everything before it's time to go home. Isn't that what life is all about? Having fun playing as hard as we can, living life to the fullest!

Why is it that when we grow up and become adults we separate work from play? Why do we try to separate having fun from making a living? "Business before pleasure," we say. "You have to work hard and earn your play time." "A full day's pay for a full day's work," we think. We are a society that has grown up to think that work is not supposed to be fun. Why is that? Why can't work be just as fun as play? Better yet, why can't work be play?

Kids don't distinguish between work and play. They have fun no matter what they do. They don't care what you call it; they are going to have fun doing it. Let's take sweeping the kitchen floor as an example. If you tell children to sweep, they will become a famous hockey player like Bobby Orr. They will pretend that dust, dirt, and food particles on the floor are a hockey puck. They pretend the chairs, table, and other furniture are opposing defenders. They skate quickly through the chairs and make a shot on goal into a dustpan. "It's good!" The game continues until they completely sweep the floor.

Picking up their clothes is another wonderful game that children play to make their work fun. They pick up their pants with five seconds left on the clock. They dribble behind their bed and eye the laundry basket across the room. All the while they are imitating the crowd counting down the clock: "five"—"four"—"three...." Just as the clock is about to run out, they shoot their pants across the room toward the clothes basket. The pants seem to drift across the room in slow motion. Just as the imaginary buzzer sounds, the pants hit the basket. If they make the shot, the crowd goes wild in celebration of winning the game. If they miss, somehow, the clock resets, and they get another chance to make the winning shot. Depending on how many clothes need to be picked up and how accurate the shooter is, determines the length of the game.

Washing the car is another great game children play. Now, I don't imagine children like to wash cars, but if they have to, they are going to make the best of it. They put on their bathing suits. They spray each other with a garden hose. They throw wet sponges and rags at each other as they run around the car, playing and having fun as they work.

What would happen if every business promoted playing in the workplace? What if there was a basketball goal in every hallway, and companies held meetings shooting hoops? What if pool tables and Ping-Pong tables were in every work area, and companies encouraged employees to take breaks and play games? What if your company had a corporate membership to a local country club and made it mandatory that employees spend one day a week playing golf or tennis. Why don't more companies do this? Because they think employees would never get any work done! Au contraire, but they would. How, you ask? By playing together they would create some of the best teams ever formed in corporate America. Just ask some of the companies that are already doing it.

Outdoor challenge camps that teach employees to work together as teams have realized this fact and have sprung up all over the country. In these daylong camps, coworkers learn through structured team activities how to work cohesively. They rope climb, repel, and maneuver through obstacle courses while playing and building trust in one another.

By encouraging employees to play together, they learn to work together. When people work together, productivity goes up, territorial boundaries come down, and people become adaptable and willing to work toward common goals. Some of the biggest business deals ever made came together on golf courses—corporate leaders playing as they worked.

What about absenteeism? Did you know that absenteeism is still one of the leading causes of lost productivity in the workplace? What do you think would happen to absenteeism if there were no distinction between work and play—if employees were encouraged to play as they work? You're right; absenteeism would decrease. Who would want to miss work if it were fun?

To most of us, Monday is a four-letter word. We are a nation that lives for the weekend. We waste our lives by wishing for the weekend to come as quickly as possible. Do you think if work and play were the same that we would live our lives this way?

Wouldn't it be something if we looked forward to Monday—if we actually couldn't wait to get back to work? Can you imagine employees that didn't have to be told what time to arrive and how late to stay? What if work was so much fun that we didn't want to take vacations; instead, we wanted to work all the time? That the distinction between the workweek and the weekend became blurry and hard to differentiate. Isn't that the way work should be?

Here is where we as adults have made our mistakes. We try to separate the two. Instead of playing and having fun all the time as a child would, we try to separate work from play. Somehow, we have indoctrinated ourselves to believe that if we are having fun, we couldn't be working. We believe that if we are laughing and having a good time, we must be goofing off. Others have made us believe that if we want to go to work and are willing to do anything to keep from missing it, there is something wrong with us. That is not the way we should live our lives.

Work is a part of life, and just like everything else, it should to be fun too! No matter what day of the week or what they may be doing, children are going to have fun. Sure, they sometimes have to do things they might not want to do, but they make the best of it and have fun while doing it. They go from one thing to the next, living life to the fullest.

Don't throw your life away wishing for the weekend. Life is already short enough. Enjoy each minute of each day to the fullest. Don't work yourself into a situation that someday you will look back on and wish you had done things differently.

If you're not playing and having fun at everything that you do, you need to reassess what you are doing and where you are going. You will never be as successful as you could have been if you are not having fun. The most successful people in the world are like children and make little distinction between work and play. They have fun at everything they do.

Make a commitment right now to have fun. Don't separate work from play, but play at everything you do. Make a game out of the paperwork you despise. Take a potential client to a baseball game to work out the details of a contract. Have a staff meeting in the park while feeding the pigeons. Conduct a job interview over a game of tennis. Make your business calls from a cell phone in the mall. Whatever you do, have fun doing it.

Start looking forward to Monday. Monday is the beginning of a new week where you can start anew. Last week is behind you. Take the good you learned from last week, forget the rest, and look forward to the challenges of the new week ahead.

Life is a playground. You have to play hard. Don't rest until you have played on everything. Remember, those who play the hardest will be the most successful.

Use Power Phrases and Words Whenever Possible

Children use the English language to their advantage whenever possible. They will take words you say, turn them around, and use them against you. They will take the real or implied meaning of a word and use the definition that best suits them. They will never forget or let you forget anything you say that will help them with their position or help them do something they want to do. Likewise, they will never remember something you said that doesn't support or help them get what they want.

Even as I write this, I remember times when my daughter used things my wife had said several days earlier to get something she wanted. As I said before, Kristen is a social child, and her wants and needs usually involved her friends. Once, my wife suggested to our daughter that if we weren't busy the following Saturday, she would take Kristen and one of her friends to the mall to go shopping. Saturday arrived, and of course, that is not what my daughter remembered. Kristen was absolutely sure that my wife had promised that she would take them to the mall no matter what was going on. According to Kristen, her mother never stated anything about their trip being dependent on anything. It was Saturday, and it was time to pick up her friend and go to the mall.

This is typical behavior for a ten-year-old. Kristen heard and remembered the parts of the conversation that supported what she wanted to do. The rest she forgot. She intentionally forgot the most important part—"if we aren't busy." Even when reminded of the exact time and location where the statement was made, she had no recollection of anything like that being said. In fact, she had no recollection of the time or place when my wife supposedly said it. Her memory was totally absent of any statement that vaguely resembled that qualifier.

Children have selective memory. They can only remember certain things. They can remember something you promised to do for them seven months ago when, at the time, you wanted to do something else. They can remember a trip to the zoo you planned for August back in January when it was twenty below zero. They can remember a birthday, spend-the-night party you casually mentioned to them at last year's birthday party. They can remember who gets to go down the slide first the next time you go to the park three months from now. I'm always amazed at what my children can remember long after I have forgotten. They can remember almost anything they think will benefit them in the future.

However, children will never remember some things. They will never remember something you've told them fourteen times in the last seven minutes. They will never remember to keep all four legs of their chair on the floor. They will never remember to put their coat on before they leave the house when it is below freezing outside. They will never remember to close the door when they use the bathroom or take a shower. They will never remember to brush their teeth unless you are standing right there beside them. Unless they see it as something that will give them some advantage in the future, they are unable to remember it. Or can they?

Just like selective memory, children sometimes have selective memory loss. This happens when they remember what you said or did, but see no advantage to themselves for admitting it. They know that admitting they remember could be detrimental to them and their plans. So, what do they do? They tell you they don't know what you are talking about. They tell you anything to steer you away from the truth. They confuse the truth by introducing unrelated issues that have very little to do with the discussion at hand. Some children are good at it. Kristen is one of them.

Fortunately, for my wife and me, Kristen did not have the art of fibbing perfected. She didn't always know when to be quiet and when to protest. She hadn't learned how to look us straight in the eyes when she told us a whopper. She didn't yet know what was believable and what was not believable to the average adult. I'm thankful her skills were not well developed. It gave her mother and me a fighting chance.

So you see, because of the knowledge I have of Kristen, I have no doubt that she remembered what her mother said. She can pretend all she wants that she didn't hear her mother make this statement, but I know she did. Kristen thought she would pull a good one on her mother by not remembering. She thought that if she pretended she didn't hear the statement being made that it would not make the statement binding. I'm sure that in her mind it made good sense. I mean how could her parents hold her to something she didn't even hear?

When Kristen realized she wasn't getting very far with her mother, she came to me. It wasn't right away. She waited until her mother left for a meeting at church before she approached me. Remember *The Equal Authority Slide*? Kristen, not knowing that I had been listening to her earlier conversation with her mother, asked me if I wanted to go to the mall with them. She told me that her mother, her friend, and herself were going to the mall and encouraged me to come along. Of course, she didn't mention the conversation with her mother. She never once mentioned her mother's stipulation of being busy.

Knowing that she didn't know I knew about their conversation, I had some fun with Kristen. I told her that I would love to go with them to the mall because I had several errands I needed to run, and I could do them while we were out. First, I told her I needed to go to the hardware store. I knew she wouldn't like it because when we go the hardware store, we walk around for hours. She screwed up her face a little bit when I said it, but she agreed. I guess she figured that to be able to go to the mall, it was worth doing one thing she didn't want to do.

Next, I told her I needed to go to the bookstore. This is another place where we spend a great deal of time looking. I could see in her face before she answered her weighing whether the trip was still worth the concessions she would have to make. Her lower jaw dropped slightly as she cocked her head a little to the side, but she agreed to go.

Finally, I mentioned the place I knew would be the last straw. I told her I needed to get my hair cut. That was it! Her eyes rolled back into her head as her frustration level went through the roof. She no longer saw any benefit in going to the mall. The time she wanted to spend walking the hallways of the mall would now be spent running errands with her dad. She left the room without saying a word.

Now if I hadn't known about her previous conversation with her mother, I might have agreed with Kristen and made arrangements to go. Then, when my wife returned from her meeting, Kristen would have met her at the door and told her that I wanted to go to the mall with them. My wife, believing that I wanted to go, may have given in, and we would have spent our afternoon at the mall. We would have once again fallen victim to *The Equal Authority Slide.*

Adults are no different when it comes to memory. Just like children, they sometimes have selective memory. They only remember what they want to remember. They have selective memory loss and sometimes can't remember what someone said just a few minutes prior. And yes, just like a child, they sometimes fib a little when they feel that remembering something will cause them not to get what they want. The maturing process unfortunately does not change our propensity to use what someone did or did not say to our advantage.

When I asked Kristen about her earlier conversation with her mom, she used the first of three power phrases on me. In her own heart, she knew she had not told the truth, and she was certain I had caught her. She knew that carrying on with the lie would only get her into more trouble. So what did she do? With the sincerity of Mother Teresa, she told me that she was sorry. Now, Kristen may not be very good at telling lies, but she is among the best at using power phrases.

Power Phrase or Word Number One: I'm Sorry!

I'm sorry is perhaps one of the most powerful phrases in the English language. When used correctly, it calms any situation. It eases emotions and allows people to work out their differences. It diffuses confrontation and allows the healing process to begin.

When you say you are sorry for something, you ask for forgiveness. You admit you have done wrong and ask for another chance. You acknowledge your inappropriate behavior and submit yourself to the wronged person. You concede your improper conduct and ask for absolution from your actions.

We all make mistakes. We all do or say things we wish we could take back. Saying "I'm sorry" is a good place to start, as it reopens productive communications to resolve issues.

Kristen knew the power of those two words. She knew that to express her thoughts and feelings about her predicament to her parents, she had to diffuse the situation, acknowledge her mistake, and submit herself to her parents. She did exactly that! She said she was sorry. She allowed the healing process to begin.

When you get into situations where you have done wrong, don't lie to cover your tracks. Say you are sorry for whatever you did and start the healing process. You will be amazed at how powerful this phrase really is.

I would be remiss in not telling you the end of this story. When confronted with her lie, she confessed and said she was sorry. Her reasons behind her actions were convincing. By saying she was sorry, she persuaded me to stop and listen to her and brought me to a new understanding of what she really wanted.

When something goes wrong, say you are sorry. It will diffuse any situation and allow others to hear your point of view. In addition, saying you are sorry will start the healing process and will allow things to get back to normal.

Did Kristen get to go to the mall with her friend? She sure did! We spent all afternoon there.

Power Phrase or Word Number Two: Please!

Please is another powerful word. The word please will open doors to you that you never dreamed would open. Something about the politeness of please opens the minds of people to your ideas.

Children know this. Listen to children when they really want something. What's the first word that comes out of their mouth? You guessed it, they say "please." If they perceive they might not get what they want, they will use this word over and over. I'm sure you remember using this word a few times when you were a child.

Kristen is a master of the word "please." She knows how to use it in every situation. She has mastered every type of speech inflection to maximize her impact. She has complete control over her body language and her tear ducts and, when combined with her use of the word please, delivers a knockout punch that very few people can withstand.

Let's look back at my previous story. When Kristen realized we had caught her in a lie, and she said she was sorry, the very next word out of her mouth was please. Kristen knew that by saying she was sorry she had my full attention, and then she went for my juggler.

"Please let me go to the mall with my friend," she asked in a humble, subdued voice. "Please let me be with my friend."

"Why should I let you go after you lied to me?" I asked.

Without saying a word, she lowered her head and looked at the floor. After a short pause, she said in the most convincing voice she had, "I'm sorry, daddy. I made a big mistake, and I am truly sorry."

As she raised her head to look me in the eyes, she pleaded, "Please let me go to the mall. You don't understand how much this means to me. All my friends are going to be there. Please?" Almost on cue, a tear slowly rolled down her cheek.

I told you she was good. What could I say? Even though I knew she lied, and I thought she was pulling my chain, I couldn't say no. Looking back on it now, I think she probably knew I couldn't say no before I even answered.

Just like Kristen, all children realize the power of the word please. They will use it whenever they need a little extra help in getting something they want. Just as you did when you were a child, you must use this powerful word to your advantage. Always lead every request with the word please. It may give you the extra help you need to get a positive response.

This leads us to the final power phrase that people usually use in conjunction with the word please—thank you!

Power Phrase or Word Number Three: Thank You!

Thank you closes a request. It shows your appreciation to others for something they have said or done. Thank you also leaves open the possibility of additional requests at a later date.

Everyone likes to be thanked. Everyone likes appreciation for something they have done. When you thank someone, it makes him or her feel good about what he or she has done for you and more willing to do something for you in the future. It also assures the one you are thanking that they are doing the right thing.

As parents, we work hard to have our children use this phrase. Every time someone does something for our children, we urge them to say thank you. "What do you say?" we ask our children when they should respond with a thank you. When they finally say it, we feel good about what our children have done.

As my children got older, and their friends visited more often, I noticed their friends saying thank you. Even if whatever they were thanking me for had inconvenienced me at the time, their words diffused the situation, and my displeasure decreased. I thought to myself how polite they were, and I hoped my kids were as polite when they were visiting their friends' homes. Am I more willing to respond to their requests in the future? You bet I am. Saying thank you demonstrates appreciation for something someone has done for you and may open up opportunities in the future.

Never miss an opportunity to say thank you to someone who has gone out of his or her way to do something for you. It shows gratitude to them for their actions and it keeps their door open for future acts of kindness.

I'm sorry, please, and thank you are powerful phrases. They elicit positive responses even when circumstances may not be so positive. They diffuse ugly situations and leave open the possibility of future requests. Success will come to you easier if you use these phrases appropriately.

Keep a Special Friend Close

I have never seen a child as afraid of the dark as my daughter Kristen. Before she went to sleep each night, she would make my wife and me go through a search–and-destroy ritual in her room. We were never quite sure what we were looking for, but she was convinced that something from the dark was going to harm her while she slept. Before we could turn off the lights, we had to look under her bed and in her closet to prove there was nothing there waiting to hurt her.

Just casually looking under the bed was not good enough for Kristen. We had to get down on our hands and knees and check every inch of floor under her bed. While we looked, she sat on the edge of her bed looking over the side, never offering to help. Once we gave her the all-clear sign, she would point us in the direction of her closet. Her closet had bi-fold doors that she urged us to open. For some reason she didn't want to look under her bed, but insisted that she personally look into her closet. As she sat on her bed, Kristen visually inspected her closet, and when she was satisfied that everything was okay, she instructed us to close the doors. If we left her room without closing the doors, she would call us back into her room, remind us to close them, and not lie down until we had.

To assure her that nothing would harm her, we accommodated her every wish. We didn't mind in any way going through this nightly ritual with her and were willing to do most anything to make her feel safe. Each night during the search, we pledged to her that we would never allow anything to hurt her and would always be there for her if she needed us.

As we turned off the lights to leave her room, Kristen would lie in the middle of her bed and, as a final act before she went to sleep, arrange her stuffed animals all around her. She systematically collected them each night and would not go to sleep until each was in its place. It still amazes us how she could have slept in the middle of such a pile of animals. Unless you looked closely, you would never know that she was hidden in the middle of them.

With a kiss on her cheek, we lovingly said good night and left her room. She lay motionless in her bed with the covers pulled up to her chin, seemingly afraid to move. We could only see her eyes moving from side to side in the middle of a large mass of fur. She blended in with her stuffed animals and became one with them.

From the moment the lights went out until the sun came up the next morning, Kristen never moved or made a sound. The position we left her in each night was the position we found her in the next morning. I believe she was so afraid of the dark that she feared moving would give her away, and the creatures of the dark would find her.

Kristen's fear of the dark was not only confined to her bedroom, but also transcended throughout every part of her life. She would not go into any room unless the light was on. It didn't matter where we were in relation to Kristen, if the light was not on in the room that she wanted to go into, she summoned us from wherever we were to turn it on. She stood at the edge of the darkness and refused to enter the room until someone turned on the light. It didn't matter to Kristen if the light switch was fifteen feet across the room or just inches away right by the door. She would not stick any part of her body into the darkness.

By the age of ten, Kristen's fear of the darkness had improved. She no longer made us look under her bed and in her closet before the lights went out. She no longer hid in the middle of her stuffed animals, afraid to move. She was no longer afraid to go into a dark room to turn on a light. However, her fear of the darkness carried on. Even several years later, she would still not go to sleep without her nightlight on.

I know what you are thinking. Kristen has a phobia about darkness, but you're wrong. She is no different from any other child. Many children are afraid of the dark at some time or another. They may not be as afraid of the dark as Kristen was, but they are afraid just the same. They are afraid of the unknown, of the darkness, and are fearful to venture into it. They are afraid of the creatures—real or imaginary—lurking in the darkness that might harm them. They are afraid of things they can hear but cannot see.

Adults, even though we don't always want to admit it, are also sometimes afraid of the dark. Producers of television shows and movies recognize this fear and incorporate our fears into their storylines every way they can. It makes programs exciting when they place actors in situations that play on our fears of the unknown. The music gets a little eerie, and when we least expect it, they startle us by bringing to life our fears of the dark.

So, where am I going with this? It's simple. There will be times in your life when you need to go into the darkness to deal with the unknown. There will be times when you face situations when you will not know what to do or where to turn. There will be times when you will face many choices and not know which one to choose. There will be times when you will need to make tough decisions and face unknown consequences. There will be times when you think there is no hope and you will be ready to give up. All of us at some point are surrounded by darkness—whether we want to admit it or not—that scares us and causes us to seek encouragement, comfort, and assurance from someone that everything will be all right.

Children overcome their fears of the darkness by having faith in their parents. They believe their parents and trust that they will always be there to protect them. They know their parents would never intentionally allow anything to harm them. Children go to their parents for comfort and assurance. In spite of the unknown of the darkness, they receive assurance that everything will be all right.

How do you overcome your fears of the darkness? Where do you get your comfort? Where do you go when darkness surrounds you, and you don't know what to do next? Where do you go for assurance that you have made the right decision when faced with many difficult choices? Where do you go for consolation when things seem hopeless and you are ready to give up? Where do you place your trust when no one seems trustworthy? Where does your strength come from when times are uncertain?

Some people get their strength and comfort from a bottle. They somehow think that they can drink their fears away. Unfortunately, their fears never go away for long. They resurface when they sober up and find themselves right where they left off.

Others put their trust in drugs. For a few minutes or hours, they chemically remove themselves from their problems. They isolate themselves from the world, trying to physically separate themselves from their fears. Just like those who drink, their problems and fears of the dark never go away for long.

Alcohol or drugs will never give you comfort from your fears. You can never place your trust in something that can't be trusted. These things will never calm your fears or solve your problems but will only lead to destruction. They make you unable to see things clearly and drive you away from those who can help you. They will not bring you out of the darkness, but will only cause you to lose sight of your dream and dash your hopes for success.

So, where should you get comfort from the darkness? Where should you place your trust for answers to difficult questions? Where should you get your strength and energy to face the unknown? Some people use a best friend, a girlfriend, a boyfriend, or a spouse. Others use a pastor or priest to share their darkest secrets and fears. Others use their parents their entire life to bounce ideas off of and to get reactions to their thoughts. Who better than your parents to keep your best interests at heart?

Wherever you look for comfort from the dark, find someone you can trust unconditionally. Find someone who can look beyond his or her own insecurities and give you honest feedback. Someone you can go to with anything that keeps you awake at night and find comfort.

For you see, sometimes you will have to walk into the darkness of the unknown, abandon all fear, and have faith that trusted someone will be there with you. From time to time, you will need answers to difficult questions and will need to seek counsel from someone who will provide unbiased opinions. Occasionally you will need the strength that you can only get from a trusted special someone who always has your back and gives you comfort that everything will be all right.

At times, we must all put our trust and confidence in someone other than ourselves. We must depend on this trusted someone to pull us through the darkness into the light on the other side. In these times of uncertainly, we must be able to turn to that special person in our life and allow them to help us work things out. They know us better than anyone else and will always have our best interests at heart.

When you find yourself surrounded by darkness and unsure of what to do or how to react, turn to your special person for guidance. That person will never let you down.

Focus on the Fundamentals to Be Successful

In summary, success is up to you. It's not up to your boss or your employer. Success is not up to your spouse or your best friend. It's not up to the luck of the draw or you winning the lottery. Success is up to you, and if you want to be successful at everything you do, you and only you can make it happen.

You already possess all the skills necessary to be successful in every aspect of your life. You have them within you today. They took shape and developed when you were a small child, and they remain with you all of your life. The choice is yours. You can either ignore these skills and refuse to use them, and let lady luck determine your success, or you can use these skills in every part of your daily life, letting the knowledge you already have within you make you successful.

Be like a child and live your dreams. Whatever you want to do, get started doing it today! Without action, a dream remains abstract and never becomes concrete but stays in the someday part of your mind. How can you expect to realize whatever you want to accomplish if you never act on it? Start today, and make your dreams come alive, not in your mind, but through your actions.

Being successful at everything you do is fundamental. Focus on the fundamental elements of success, and success will come naturally. Success is not difficult. Everyone can be successful. You have already been successful a million times over to this point in your life.

Unlike children, adults try to make being successful much harder than it really is. As a result, we never try. We talk ourselves out of getting started. Children never give up before they start. You didn't as a child, and you shouldn't let it happen as an adult. You can be successful at everything!

What does it take to be successful? You must simplify the process by only focusing on the fundamentals of success—the building blocks of success. When you break success down into its simplest form, remember there are seven fundamental elements that you must focus on.

First, you must commit yourself to be successful. You have gotta want it more than anything else, and make it a top priority in your life. Success is not difficult, but no one will ever just hand it to you on a platter. If you want to be successful at everything you do, you have to fight for it. You must always do you best work, and never lose focus on your goals.

Unlike it was when we were children, as adults we don't focus on the possibility of succeeding but focus on the possibility of failing. The biggest challenge we face in becoming successful is ourselves. We are our own worst enemies. We let memories of past failures clutter our minds and keep us from trying. We try to predict our future failures before we even start. We let others talk us out of trying things when they ridicule us about our ideas. We tell ourselves that we are under-qualified to do certain tasks, and instead of learning the skills we need or surrounding ourselves with people who have the skills we require, we give up before we even begin. If we do finally get started, we over-plan everything we do. We plan and plan, and at some point the planning becomes more important than our goal, and we lose interest.

The first step in every success is getting started. You have to get up out of your comfortable chair and do something. Even if you go down the wrong path at first, every path will eventually lead to success if you will only start walking. It may not be the shortest path to where you want to go, but if you want it bad enough, any path you take will ultimately lead to your final destination. Getting started and moving down the path toward your goal is the first step in being successful at anything.

When you were a child, you never let anything get in the way of something you wanted to do. You didn't let memories of past failure stop you from doing something. You didn't try to predict what problems you might encounter along the way; you took a chance and moved forward with your plans. You didn't let someone—not even your parents—talk you out of doing something if you really wanted to do it. Nothing could stop you. You never worried about being qualified. Education, title, or status didn't mean anything to you. You did whatever you wanted to do. Being qualified never entered your mind. Planning was never an issue either. You planned as you went. When you encountered a problem, you quickly moved in a new direction, never keeping it from distracting you from your goal. You kept moving forward never looking back.

Now that you are an adult, the same rules apply. If you want something, you have got to fight for it just as you did when you were a child. Nothing has changed from then until now. If you want to be successful at everything you do, you must commit yourself to your goal, want it bad enough to get started, and make it a top priority in your life.

Second, you must believe in yourself. If you don't believe you can be successful, you probably will never reach your full potential. Success breeds success. When you believe in yourself and as more successes come to you, you simplify your path of future successes by building on past accomplishments.

Growing up, you were invincible. There wasn't anything that you didn't think you could do. From the moment you were born, your parents began to convince you that you could do anything. Guess what? You believed them. Every step of your maturing process your parents continued to encourage you, and over time, you believed you could accomplish anything.

Somewhere between childhood and adulthood, we begin to doubt ourselves and lose the confidence we once had as children. Why is that? At some point in our lives, we begin to listen to the people around us who play on our fear of failure. Worse yet, we begin to believe them, and it shatters our confidence.

There will always be people trying to stand in the way of you being successful. There will always be people trying to play on your insecurities and keep you from reaching your goals. These people will come to you as a good friend, a coworker, a parent, or a spouse and, yes, even a complete stranger. By destroying your confidence in yourself, they get pleasure from feeling better about themselves when you don't succeed. Don't give these people pleasure by letting them attack your confidence. Keep them away from you, your dreams, and your ideas.

Just as you did when you were a child, you must block these people from your life. Block out all distractions they present to you, and stay focused on your goals. You must have the confidence you once had as a child, and believe you can do anything you set your mind to. You've done it before; you must do it again. Having confidence in your ability to succeed is the second fundamental element of success.

Third, you must have a winning attitude. A winning attitude is not a positive attitude but a state of mind. When you encounter failures, you pick yourself up after a brief moment of disappointment, brush yourself off, and try again.

No one can be positive all the time. Life happens, and it will knock us down at times when we least expect it. There are always going to be things that happen that won't make us feel very positive. We know maintaining a positive attitude all the time is impossible and unrealistic. In fact, we know from experience that just being positive will not make us successful. To be successful in everything we do, we must have a winning attitude.

What is a winning attitude? A winning attitude acknowledges that many things will cause us to stumble and fall. It also realizes that during these times, we are not going to be very positive. But a winning attitude differs from a positive attitude in that, with a winning attitude, no matter what happens or how bad things get, we acknowledge our frustration, pick ourselves up, brush ourselves off, and try again. That's a winning attitude.

As a child, you didn't let every little obstacle that got into your way stop you from doing something you wanted to do. When things didn't go the way you thought they should, you didn't quit and give up. You tried something different. You didn't look for someone else to blame when things went wrong. You picked yourself up, brushed yourself off, and tried again. That's what someone with a winning attitude does.

Now that you are an adult, nothing has changed. Just as you did when you were a child, when things go wrong, get mad if you want to but never for long. Pick yourself up, brush yourself off, and try again. You must have an attitude that is not afraid to fail but accepts failure as a part of life. An attitude that is not afraid to get mad or be negative, but when things go wrong within a short period, is willing to forget the disappointment and move on. You must have an attitude that doesn't look for someone else to blame but blames yourself for your failures. An attitude that doesn't quit at the first sign of trouble, but picks yourself up, brushes yourself off, and tries again and again until you are finally successful. If you want to be successful at everything you do, you must focus on the third fundamental element of success and maintain a winning attitude.

Fourth, you must be adaptable. You must be willing to change with the wind, and adapt to whatever life throws at you. Success is a moving target. It doesn't sit still and wait for you, nor can you sit still and wait for it. It is a constantly moving target. To be successful at everything you do, you must be willing to move with it.

When you were a child, you, like all children, were a master of change and adaptability. Within a few short years, you developed and adapted to meet every challenge you faced. You learned to walk and talk. You learned to feed yourself and change your own clothes. You learned to control you bodily functions as you adapted to the world around you. As a child, you took every challenge in stride. You changed and adapted to whatever life threw at you.

As an adult, just as you did when you were a child, you must adapt to everything that life throws at you. Your success depends on it. The next time life throws a curve ball at you, look at it as you did when you were a child, and create an opportunity, not a problem. Life is too short to create problems. You must be willing to change at the drop of a hat, adjust, and take advantage of every opportunity of life. Life is full of opportunities for those who are willing to adapt and change to meet them. Therefore, adaptability is the fourth fundamental element of being successful.

Fifth, you must never stop learning. Knowledge is power. The more knowledge you have about anything the more power and insight you will have to help you make sound decisions in all phases of your life. The learning process is the same today as it was when you were a child.

How did we all learn new things as children? Children learn about their world in four ways: they break things, they learn from their mistakes, they learn from other successful children, and if they don't know something, they ask. These are the same methods you used when you were a child and are the same techniques you should be using to learn all the things you need to know to be successful as an adult. Learning everything you can is not only a fundamental element of the building blocks of success, it also gives you the power and knowledge you need and will allow you to be successful at everything you do.

To know the things you need to know, sometimes just like you did when you were a child, you have to break things. You have to tear things apart piece by piece and see how they work. You have to get deep into the weeds and touch and feel every part to see how something is put together. Don't be afraid to break something if it gives you the knowledge you need.

Children learn from their mistakes; so must you. Don't look at mistakes negatively, but take them as a vehicle of learning that will carry you down the quickest road to success. You must accept that mistakes are a part of life. No one has accomplished anything worthwhile without making mistakes and learning from them. Don't be afraid of making mistakes, but cherish them for the knowledge they give you.

A child learns from other successful children. Like when you were a child, don't be afraid to use the skills and knowledge of others to help you overcome your obstacles. Identify the people around you who can help you succeed. Surround yourself with their knowledge and learn from their mistakes so that you don't have to experience them. Most people are happy and willing to help you succeed if you will only ask them.

If children don't know something, they ask. If you don't know something, don't be afraid to ask. You weren't afraid to ask when you were a child. Why should you be afraid now? Use questions to your advantage, because if you don't ask, you will never know. And if you never know the things you need to know, success will be difficult if not impossible to achieve. Success comes to those who question everything and are never satisfied until they know the answers to all their questions.

A child never stops learning, but lives to learn new things. Now that you are an adult, you must remain committed to learning. To be successful at everything you do, you can never stop learning. You can never be satisfied with just what you know, but must learn everything you can. You can never dismiss or discard any new idea, but must learn whatever you can from it. Knowledge is truly the most powerful tool that you have, and you must always use it to your advantage.

The sixth fundamental element of success is being able to think outside the lines. Not being bound by imaginary boundaries that are sometimes drawn around us is critical to finding solutions to problems that sometimes seem unsolvable. As in most cases in life, the only boundaries we really have are the limits we place on ourselves. When you remove these limits, success quickly follows.

As children, we easily stepped outside the lines of normal thinking to do something we really wanted to do. This kind of thinking is what made you successful as a child, and it will make you successful as an adult if you will only do it.

Why do adults have trouble thinking outside the lines? Why do we allow the boundaries we place around ourselves to hold us captive and prevent us from conquering the many opportunities around us? Our problem starts from the moment that we can hold a crayon in our hand and we color the first picture.

Coloring pictures is a fun activity. Kids of all ages love to color and, if allowed, will color for hours at a time. By picking just the right color and applying it in just the right spots, they make the picture come alive. Their imaginations run rampant to satisfy their creativity and to produce something beautiful.

Then it happens. They get their first instruction in the art of coloring. "No honey! You need to stay inside the lines," a well-meaning adult instructs them. From that moment forward, they never look at lines or boundaries the same way. Others program them to think that going outside the lines is not acceptable, which lessens the value of creativity. This line of reasoning continues throughout their teen years and stays with them even as adults.

It's not easy to think outside the lines. It's not easy to try new and different ideas. What if someone questions your idea or, worse yet, makes fun of it? No one wants to be made fun of or laughed at. But sometimes you have to take a chance. You have to think outside the lines to solve difficult problems. You have to use ideas you have never used before. To be successful at everything you do, sometimes it will be necessary for you to step outside the lines, and try new things you may have never tried before.

Don't be afraid to think outside the lines. Don't be afraid to take a chance. Don't be afraid to knock down the boundaries that you or others may have placed around you. Just like you did when you were a child, don't be afraid to cross the line.

To be successful, you have to think outside the lines. You have to be able to recognize the boundary lines and always be willing to cross them. To solve the most difficult problems, you sometimes have to look past the obvious and traditional ways of thinking, and visualize the untapped possibilities that are on the other side of the line. Success is easy to those who can think outside the lines and see the opportunities on the other side.

The seventh and final fundamental element of success is making sure you tell everyone about your dreams and goals. As unbelievable as it may seem, there are people in this world that want to help you be successful. Family, friends, colleagues, and sometimes even complete strangers are more than willing to help you get what you want. But to provide people you have contact with the opportunity to help you, you must tell them about your dreams. You must express what you want with anyone who will listen.

Think back to when you were a child. When you wanted something, did you keep it a secret? Of course not, you told everyone that you came in contact with. I don't care what it was that you wanted or how silly it may have seemed, if you wanted something, you told whoever would listen.

As adults, we tend to keep what we want to ourselves. Oh, we may tell a few close friends or a spouse, but as a general rule, we keep it to ourselves, and never tell anyone. Why do adults keep secrets about what we want? Is it because we are afraid of what people may think about us? Are we afraid others may laugh at or ridicule our ideas? Are we afraid people will discount our ideas and tell us we are wasting our time? Generally, for all those who may be negative towards us, there will be many more that will want to help us.

Just like a child, adults have nothing to lose by telling people what they want. If you want something, you not only have to work hard for it, but you have to ask for it as well. You will rarely have what you want handed to you. You have to let people know what you want, and allow them to help you get it.

If children want something, they will let you know about it immediately. They don't hold back. They don't keep it a secret from anyone. They are not afraid to ask for whatever they want and will use any opportunity do it. Children know instinctively that if they don't ask for what they want, there is no way they will ever get it. They know that if they want something, they have to let the people around them know about it.

To be successful at everything you do, you must tell everyone your goals and dreams. You can't hold back or keep secrets from anyone. You have to plant your seed or idea in their mind, sit back, and let it grow and flourish. You have to make your dreams come alive in their mind, knowing that someday, someone will take action on your behalf. Someone is waiting to help you. Tell everyone you know, and enjoy the success you achieve.

These are the seven fundamental elements of being successful and are truly the building blocks of success. If you focus on these basic elements, no matter what you may attempt in life, they will make you successful at everything you do.

However, you must remember three more things vital to success, and use them in conjunction with the seven fundamental elements. They are: have fun doing everything you do, use power phrases or words whenever possible, and keep a special friend close.

First and foremost, life was meant to be fun. Whatever you do, make sure you have fun doing it. Like a wise man once said, if you do what you like, and have fun doing it, you will never work another day in your life. I don't know about you, but I think that is pretty good advice.

As adults we have indoctrinated ourselves to believe that if we are having fun we couldn't be working. We believe that if we are laughing and having a good time, we must be goofing off. Stop this kind of thinking!

Don't throw your life away wishing for the weekend. Life is already short enough. Live and enjoy to the fullest each minute of every day. Don't work yourself into a situation that someday you will look back on and wish you had handled differently.

If you're not playing and having fun at everything that you do, you need to reassess what you are doing and where you are going. You will never be as successful as you could have been if you are not having fun. Just like you had fun doing everything you did when you were a child, the most successful people in the world make no distinction between work and play. They have fun at everything they do.

Second, use power phrases and words to help you be successful. "I'm sorry," "please," and "thank you" are powerful phrases that elicit positive responses, even when the circumstances may not be so positive. Use them whenever possible to diffuse bad situations, to ask for forgiveness, to solicit help when a task is beyond your understanding or skill, and to acknowledge your appreciation for the help someone has given you.

When you say you are sorry for something, you ask for forgiveness. You admit you have done wrong, and ask for another chance. You acknowledge your inappropriate behavior, and submit yourself to the wronged person. You concede your improper conduct, and ask for absolution from your actions.

We all make mistakes. We all do or say things we wish we could take back. Saying "I'm sorry" is a good place to start and reopens productive communications.

When something goes wrong, say you're sorry. You used this word every chance you got to ask for forgiveness when you were a child. It will work for you as an adult, too. Saying you're sorry will diffuse any situation and allow your point of view to be heard. In addition, saying you're sorry will start the healing process and allow things to get back to normal.

"Please" is another powerful word. The word please will open up doors to you that you never dreamed would open. Something about the politeness of the word may open the minds of people to your ideas.

Children know this. Listen to children when they really want something. What's the first word that comes out of their mouth? You guessed it, they say please. If they perceive things are not going well, and they might not get what they want, they use this word repeatedly. I'm sure you remember using this word a few times when you were a child, don't you?

All children realize the power of the word please. They will use it whenever they need a little extra help in getting something they want. Just as you did when you were a child, you must use this powerful word to your advantage. Always lead every request with the word please. It may give you the extra help you need to get a positive response.

The final power phrase or word is "thank you." This phrase is used to close a request. It shows appreciation to others for something they have said or done. Thank you also leaves open the possibility of additional requests at a later date.

Everyone likes to be thanked. Everyone likes to be appreciated for something they've done. When you thank someone, it makes them more willing to do something else for you in the future. It also assures the one being thanked that they are doing the right thing.

Like you learned as a child, never miss an opportunity to thank others who have gone out of their way to do something for you. It shows gratitude to them for their actions and keeps their door open for future acts of kindness.

"I'm sorry," "please," and "thank you" are powerful phrases. They elicit positive responses, even when circumstances may not be so positive. They diffuse ugly situations and leave open the possibility of future requests. Success will come to you more easily if you use these phrases appropriately.

The third and final thing that must be remembered and used in conjunction with the seven fundamentals of success is always keep a special friend close. For you see, sometimes you will face difficult choices that will force you to walk into the darkness of the unknown and abandon all fear. From time to time, you will need answers to difficult questions and will need to seek counsel from someone who will provide unbiased opinions. Occasionally you will need the strength that you can only get from a trusted special someone who always has your back and gives you comfort, reassuring you that everything will be all right.

At times throughout our lives, we must all put our trust and confidence in someone other than ourselves. During these times, we must depend on this trusted someone to pull us through the darkness into the light on the other side. In these times of uncertainly, we must be able to turn to that special person in our lives and allow him or her to help us work things out. That person knows us better than anyone else and will always have our best interests at heart.

When you find yourself surrounded by darkness and unsure of what to do or how to react, turn to your special person for guidance. He or she will never let you down.

There you have it. Focusing on the fundamental elements of being successful gives you all the skills and knowledge you need to be successful at everything you do. They are truly the building blocks of success.

We control our success. We make the decisions and determine the paths we follow. We are responsible—good and bad—for the ultimate outcome of our lives. Whether we are successful at life and able to follow our dreams depends on us and no one else.

What do you want to do? Who do you want to be? What makes you happy? What gets you excited about life? What is holding you back from following your dreams?

If you don't remember anything else, remember these two things. First, get started! This is the most important thing you can do, and it is always the first step in becoming successful at anything. Quit thinking about what you are going to do someday and get started doing it. Second, never give up! No matter what happens, what setbacks you encounter, or what mistakes you make, you must never give up. You must always stay focused and push forward toward your dream.

What are you waiting on? You have all the tools you need to be successful. You've had them since you were a small child.

Being successful at anything in life is not difficult. In fact, it is scary how simple it really is when you fully understand what it takes to be successful. When you break success down into its fundamental elements and begin to focus on the things that are really important to being successful, success comes easily.

Not only is being successful easy once you understand what is involved, anyone can be successful. Success doesn't depend on your socioeconomic status, nationality, gender, or race. If you have a good idea or dream you want to develop or follow, and you pay close attention to the fundamentals of success, you can be successful at anything.

When we break the fundamentals of success down into its most basic elements, it unclutters the process and simplifies our path to success. How does it do this? We falsely believe that to be successful at anything, the process has to be complicated. Simplicity is the key to everything in life. The simpler anything is, the easier it is to achieve. Keeping the process as simple as we can by breaking it down into its most fundamental elements, as we have done here, is the key to being successful at everything.

Yesterday is gone forever. Tomorrow may never come. Today is all we are promised. What you do today will determine your success now and in the future. Get started! Use the fundamental elements of success to help you become successful at everything you do. This is what I hope for you.

Epilogue

People ask me all the time about two things: what are Jonathan and Kristen doing now, and what are my dreams? First, let me say that I am a very proud papa of two terrific children, who have grown up and are moving toward successful careers of their own. Jonathan has stayed focused, never wavered on his dream, has completed his PhD in aerospace engineering, and is working in the industry as a researcher. Kristen, like her dad in many ways, has finished her undergraduate work in psychology, is following a new dream, and is pursuing a career in business. You guessed it, in the pet store industry. Jonathan and Kristen are doing wonderful, and they both make their mother and me very proud.

What do I dream about? My dreams have never really been about myself. My dreams have always been about listening to and encouraging others to find and follow their dreams. I used to think it was a curse. It seemed like someone was always telling me about his or her troubles and missed opportunities. At times, other people's trials, their unfulfilled dreams, and my desire to help them overburdened me. I guess I just have the face that everyone feels comfortable telling his or her innermost thoughts to.

It wasn't until much later in my life that I discovered my gift of listening and encouragement. My wife, Mary, was instrumental in helping me discover what I now think is my purpose in life: to encourage and help people follow their dreams.

This is what I hope for you. I hope this book will help you discover and act on your dreams. As a child, you learned every skill you will need to be successful as an adult. It is my hope that you will rediscover the child within you, and allow the skills you learned as a child help you move toward the life you have always dreamed about.

Dreams are to be lived. Allow your dreams to move from the someday part of your mind to a priority in your life. Walk without fear into the darkness as you embark on accomplishing your dreams and living the life that, up until now, you have only dreamed about.

About the Author

Bobby G. Muse, Jr. has over thirty years of business experience as a business owner, consultant, and leader. He has held responsible leadership roles in private, government, and Fortune 100 and 500 public organizations. Bobby is a graduate of the University of North Alabama in Florence, Alabama, and holds degrees in accounting and business management. In addition, he holds professional certifications in the information management and business continuity fields.

Bobby is married to his high school sweetheart, Mary, whom he met while sitting across the aisle from her in the fourth grade. They have been happily married for thirty-three years and have two wonderful children, Jonathan and Kristen, who are now embarking on successful careers of their own and were the inspiration for this book.

www.ingramcontent.com/pod-product-compliance
Lightning Source LLC
LaVergne TN
LVHW020635100826
845148LV00012B/2185

* 9 7 8 0 6 1 5 7 4 1 3 9 0 *